CONCILIUM

CONCILIUM
ADVISORY COMMITTEE

GREGORY BAUM	*Montreal, QC* Canada
JOSÉ OSCAR BEOZZO	*São Paulo, SP* Brazil
WIM BEUKEN	*Louvain* Belgium
LEONARDO BOFF	*Petrópolis, RJ* Brazil
JOHN COLEMAN	*Los Angeles, CA* USA
CHRISTIAN DUQUOC	*Lyon* France
VIRGIL ELIZONDO	*San Antonio, TX* USA
SEAN FREYNE	*Dublin* Ireland
CLAUDE GEFFRÉ	*Paris* France
NORBERT GREINACHER	*Tübingen* Germany
GUSTAVO GUTIÉRREZ	*Lima* Peru
HERMANN HÄRING	*Tübingen* Germany
WERNER G. JEANROND	*Glasgow* Scotland
JEAN-PIERRE JOSSUA	*Paris* France
MAUREEN JUNKER-KENNY	*Dublin* Ireland
FRANÇOIS KABASELE LUMBALA	*Kinshasa* Dem. Rep. of Congo
NICHOLAS LASH	*Cambridge* England
MARY-JOHN MANANZAN	*Manila* Philippines
ALBERTO MELLONI	*Reggio Emilia* Italy
NORBERT METTE	*Münster* Germany
DIETMAR MIETH	*Tübingen* Germany
JÜRGEN MOLTMANN	*Tübingen* Germany
TERESA OKURE	*Port Harcourt* Nigeria
ALOYSIUS PIERIS	*Kelaniya, Colombo* Sri Lanka
DAVID POWER	*Washington, D.C.* USA
GIUSEPPE RUGGIERI	*Catania* Italy
PAUL SCHOTSMANS	*Louvain* Belgium
JANET MARTIN SOSKICE	*Cambridge* England
ELSA TAMEZ	*San José* Costa Rica
CHRISTOPH THEOBALD	*Paris* France
DAVID TRACY	*Chicago, IL* USA
MARCIANO VIDAL	*Madrid* Spain
ELLEN VAN WOLDE	*Tilburg* Holland

CONCILIUM 2012/3

VATICAN II

Edited by

Silvia Scatena, Dennis Gira, Jon Sobrino and
Maria Clara Bingemer

SCM Press · London

Published in 2012 by SCM Press, 3rd Floor, Invicta House, 108–114 Golden Lane, London EC1Y 0TG.

SCM Press is an imprint of Hymns Ancient & Modern Ltd (a registered charity) 13A Hellesdon Park Road, Norwich NR6 5DR, UK

Copyright © International Association of Conciliar Theology, Madras (India)

www.concilium.in

English translations copyright © 2012 Hymns Ancient & Modern Ltd.

All rights reserved. No part of this publication may be reproduced, stored in a retrieval system, or transmitted, in any form or by any means, electronic, mechanical, photocopying or otherwise, without the prior written permission of the Board of Directors of Concilium.

ISBN 9780334031192

Printed in the UK by
CPI Antony Rowe, Chippenham, Wiltshire

Concilium is published in March, June, August, October, December

Contents

Editorial   7
Vatican II: Fifty Years Later

Part One: Contexts

Speechless about Vatican II?   15
PETER HŰNERMANN

Roncalli and 'his' Council   27
ALBERTO MELLONI

Vatican II as Church Enacted   36
GIUSEPPE RUGGIERI

Ressourcement and Reform at Vatican II   47
JOHN W. O'MALLEY

Vatican II Confronts the Unknown:
Collegial Discernment of the 'Signs of the Times'   56
CHRISTOPH THEOBALD SJ

Vatican II Between Catholicism and Catholicity   64
GÉRARD SIEGWALT

The Church of the Poor did not Prosper at Vatican II   75
JON SOBRINO

The Council and the Emergence of the Laity   85
MARIA CLARA BINGEMER

Part Two: Theological Forum

Look Back to the Future: Transformative Impulses of Vatican II for African Catholicism   97
AGBONHIANMEGHE E. OROBATOR

North American 'Impulses' Following Vatican II   103
MARY E. HINES

Vatican II Fifty Years Later in Latin America and the Caribbean   110
JOSE OSCAR BEOZZO

The Reception of Vatican II in a Multireligious Continent   116
FELIX WILFRED

Vatican II: Inspiration and Encouragement for the Church in Europe   122
MARTIN MAIER SJ

Comments on a Notification   129
ANDRÉS TORRES QUEIRUGA

Contributors   137

Editorial
Vatican II: Fifty Years Later

Another special issue on Vatican II? Isn't there a risk that the fiftieth anniversary of the beginning of the Council might become merely a routine occasion for celebratory reflections, nostalgically directed towards the past, or for the airing of grievances on the missed opportunities, suppressions and betrayals of Vatican II? On the other hand, today the Council question, 'that is, the question of the role, the scope and the setbacks of Vatican II in the lives of Christians and their relationships with others',[1] has become more relevant than ever. Following the revocation of the excommunication of the Lebfebvrist traditionalists in January 2009, could a journal created for the purpose of giving the conciliar Church tools for analysis and reflection *not* enquire into the significance of that event in the life of the contemporary Church?

These are some of the questions we faced when we were planning this issue. This was particularly in view of the changes that have occurred in the overall climate of the Church over the seven years since the last issue of this journal devoted to Vatican II in the autumn of 2005, the fortieth anniversary of its conclusion. We wanted to stress the Council's epoch-making value and ground-breaking nature within and between generations.[2] That was because of the widespread temptation to deny the scope of an event which changed the face of the Catholic Church, and because various forms of reductionism are at work. Firstly, there is that which avoids explicit refutation of the traditionalists, thus belittling the Council to a post-Tridentine normality, downgrading its statements on the pretext that Vatican II was a 'minor' council, because it was pastoral. Hence this issue of *Concilium* was designed to engage with the historicization of the last Council, especially with reference to certain topics and aspects singled out as especially sensitive and delicate.

When the fortieth anniversary issue came out, on the eve of Benedict XVI's well-known address about Council hermeneutics to the Roman curia on 22 December 2005, the first signs of the spread of 'normalizing' readings of Vatican II were already apparent. With the completion of the projected history of Vatican II directed by Giuseppe Alberigo, there seemed to be an attempt to relativize, not only the importance of Council history, but Vatican II itself. This betrayed the fear that the memory of that event, of its choices and even the fact that it had actually happened, might still be able to 'speak' for the present and future of the Church.[3] Those signs appearing in 2005 and, of course, the new emphases of Benedict XVI's papacy in the interpretation of the Council (from his 2005 speech to the July 2007 *motu proprio* 'Summorum Pontificum' on the liturgy) have given increased momentum to that type of reductive and minimizing reading of the significance of Vatican II, especially at the level of non-specialized theological studies, but not only there. There is widespread talk of an abstract polarity between continuity and reform versus discontinuity and breaking with the previous tradition. This is variously declined with the dialectic between the event and the final decisions, and the less recent one between the letter and spirit of the Council.[4]

In recent years, the scholarly debate about the history of the Council has made significant progress, especially in bringing together historical reconstruction and analysis of doctrinal changes and a reinterpretation of the unity of the Council *corpus*.[5] Nevertheless, the hermeneutics of Benedict XVI and the acts of his papacy have appeared to go hand-in-hand both with the recent reductionism of Vatican II in the name of the Council's continuity with 'tradition', and with the activism of an anti-conciliar revanchism. That trend was initially met with the argument of continuity as against the Lefebvrist view that Vatican II broke with catholicity.[6] The editors of this issue of Concilium did not want to ignore that context and that background, and Peter Hünermann's opening article discusses them. However, our intentions were not to enter into the more recent debate on the hermeneutics of Vatican II, or to respond to the abstract dichotomy that has been noted above, which has often seemed to be a sort of *damnatio memoriae* of the actual event of the Council.

Instead, realizing its significance as a turning point, and one which has irrevocably changed the Church's consciousness from what went before, we wanted to start positively with a reminder (which has an Augustinian intensity as 'the presence of the past') of how it began, and what was at the heart of that change which subsequently fed into the various acts of the Council. We refer to the intuition and intentions of John XXIII, who wanted that Council to bring the Gospel, though always the same in its saving eloquence, to the men and women of his own time.[7]

Although the problems and the challenges of the early 1960s are very different from those of today, nevertheless we thought it would be helpful to encourage reflection on the beginning of that event, its salient features and the fundamental attitudes impressed by Pope John XXIII on the Council. So we considered, in particular, the liberating effect that Roncalli's opening speech to the Council on 11 October 1962 had on the assembly of bishops and the Christian *oikoumene*. With the lack of hope that seems to characterize the current situation, we thought it might be helpful to understand what enabled the Catholic Church then to rediscover its own creative energies and an unexpected power to speak to contemporary humanity. Who was that Pope? And what sort of Council was Vatican II? These are the questions which two of our contributors, Alberto Melloni and Giuseppe Ruggieri, set out to answer. One concentrates on some fundamental elements of Roncalli's spirituality, which became the 'living nerves' of what in his pontificate was to be known as *aggiornamento*. The other considers the nature of a 'pastoral' Council. He interprets the ecclesiological significance, first and foremost, of Vatican II as a *representatio* of a whole Church engaged in listening to the living word of the Gospel in its own historical moment.

Aggiornamento was a typical word in Roncalli's vocabulary; it had strong universal resonance and became used without translation in various languages to indicate for a time the method and purpose of the Council. The next two contributors to this issue write about two aspects of *aggiornamento*. These are two protagonists of the more recent stage of historical and hermeneutical studies of Vatican II. They are John W. O'Malley and Christoph Theobald. The former reflects on the significance of 'ressourcement' and the Council's use of this expression. The latter looks at the other fundamental matter in the process of *aggiornamento* – the collegial discernment of the 'signs of the times'. From the papal bull summoning Vatican II on 25 December 1961, this runs like a red thread throughout the works of the Council.

We asked a Protestant voice, that of Gérard Siegwalt, for a reflection on another essential element of the Roncallian Council, the drive for unity, in many ways intrinsic to the 'pastoral' principle. This raised discussion of 'doctrinal' ecumenism, urging a more global effort in the search for unity. In the current ecumenical outlook, hope for unity seems ever more distant.

Editorial

Siegwalt focuses on the trend towards an 'inclusive' catholicity as the principal novelty of Vatican II. He contrasts an exclusivist theology of 'delimitation' with a theology of 'recapitulation'. That novelty is a challenge still to be met, not only for Roman Catholicism but for the various Protestant families and for the Orthodox.

Jon Sobrino concentrates on Roncalli's call to make the Church of the poor a decisive reason for the Council, a call which remained substantially unanswered at Vatican II. Sobrino reflects on the importance of how the theme of poverty was taken up at the Medellín Conference, an isolated exception to the widespread silence on the relevant passages of *Lumen Gentium*. These passages were the only Council response to John XXIII's initial invitation to see poverty as a central concern of the Gospel, with a strong connection between the presence of Christ in the poor and his presence in the Church. In fact, Medellín succeeded in translating the Council impulse into the 'breakthrough' of a Church of the poor, a Church which has also frequently suffered persecution and martyrdom. In an issue of *Concilium* intended to start from the 'nucleus' of what was new in the Council, we thought we had to have a contribution expressly dedicated to a prayer that, from October 1962, made its own breakthrough in the Council chamber, urging its own concerns, either relative to some of the hottest topics on the agenda of Vatican II, or for the recognition of its own space and role in the Church as the people of God.

The last article in the first part of this issue focuses on the emergence of the laity, including many important lay-people who played such a decisive part in the Councils of the first millennium and later in the Middle Ages. In her article, Maria Clara Bingemer assesses the conciliar magisterium on the laity and proposes some developments and obstacles to be overcome. Here we made an exception in this issue to the plan of having a theological forum not thematically contiguous with the monographic section. In this case, we decided that a 'topical' account of the lines of force in the Council from John XXIII's 'beginning' had to go together with a panorama of the dynamisms triggered in the churches on various continents, for which Vatican II became more a condition of their existence than an argument for debate.

With various viewpoints (some focusing on the first phases of the Council's reception, others more on the prospects and challenges today), the contributions of Agbonkhianmeghe Orobator, Mary Hines, José Beozzo, Felix Wilfred and Martin Maier try to restore some of the creative

Editorial

energies liberated by the conciliar 'new Pentecost', as Vatican II was called by the Pope who summoned it. This is not a comprehensive survey, and space was limited, so these contributions do not claim to give a sort of mini-synthesis of the planetary reception of Vatican II. We have only tried to show how the *aggiornamento* desired by Pope John was actually put into practice in the search for new ways of preaching the Gospel in different circumstances, and the impulses that it generated in different latitudes of the Catholic *oikoumene*. Some of these impulses have gone beyond what they received from the Council and others have come to a standstill and need to be revitalized.

This issue of *Concilium* was already complete, when we heard about the Notification on some works of Professor Andrés Torres Queiruga, published by the Commission for the Doctrine of Faith of the Spanish Bishops' Conference on 30 March 2012. Its purported aim was to 'safeguard essential aspects of the doctrine of the Church to avoid confusion among the People of God'. We were greatly saddened both by the arguments and the unacceptable way of presenting the decades-long work of our colleague Andrés Torres Queiruga and his efforts to present a *ratio fidei* in a culturally very complex society. We were also saddened that the way in which this was done did not give him any effective chance for dialogue or to defend himself. We thought it right to give space in the theological forum of this issue to some Comments on the Notification by our theologian friend Queiruga. He is one of the most prestigious Spanish theologians and one of the best-known internationally. In this issue dedicated to the fiftieth anniversary of Vatican II, it is also a way of expressing the dismay of the whole *Concilium* board that once again the fruit of an intelligence placed in the service of the faith has been read in an over-simplified, censorious way that is altogether lacking in good fellowship.

Silvia Scatena, Dennis Gira, Jon Sobrino, Maria Clara Bingemer
Translated by Dinah Livingstone

Notes

1. Cf. G. Miccoli, *La Chiesa dell'anticoncilio. I tradizionalisti alla riconquista di Roma*, Rome & Bari, 2011, p. 5.
2. Cf. C. Théobald, 'Vatican II: A Forgotten Future?', *Concilium*, 2005/4.
3. Cf. A. Melloni & G. Ruggieri (eds), *Chi ha paura del Vaticano II?*, Rome, 2009; M. Faggioli, *Vatican II. The Battle of the Meaning*, Manhwah, NJ, 2012; *La Storia del*

Editorial

concilio Vaticano II (1959–1965), vols 1–5, has appeared in Italian, English, French, German, Spanish, Portuguese and Russian editions.
4. See in this respect the considerations expressed by M. Faggioli at the recent seminar *1962–2012: Vatican II fifty years later. Contributions and Perspectives of the Studies on the Council ten years after the History of Vatican II*, held at Modena from 23 to 25 February 2012. The proceedings are in the course of publication.
5. See especially: H. J. Hilberath & P. Hünermann (eds), *Herders Theologischer Kommentar zum Zweiten Vatikanischen Konzil*, vols 1–5, Freiburg im Breisgau, 2004–5; J. W. O'Malley, *What Happened at Vatican II?*, Cambridge, MA, 2008; C. Théobald, *La réception du concile Vatican II, I. Accéder à la source*, Paris, 2009.
6. M. Faggioli, *Vatican II. The Battle of the Meaning*, op. cit.
7. See especially: G. Alberigo, 'Giovanni XXIII e il Vaticano II' and 'Il Vaticano II nella tradizione conciliare', in G. Alberigo, *Transizione epocale. Studi sul Concilio Vaticano II* (A. Melloni, ed.), Bologna, 2009, pp. 95–134, 553–74.

Part One: Contexts

Speechless about Vatican II?

PETER HŰNERMANN

People become speechless when they find a situation or an event so alien and incomprehensible that they are struck dumb in that respect. This kind of speech block seems to be increasing with regard to Vatican II; so much so that it seems appropriate to examine the phenomenon on the basis of actual examples.

I Three types of speech block about Vatican II

The results of the discussions between the traditionalist Society of St Pius X and the Vatican commission have clearly reached stalemate. Speaking at a January 2012 ordination service, Bishop Bernard Fellay, the leader of the dissident priests' association founded by Archbishop Lefebvre, said that in subsequent negotiations with the Roman commission they had indeed arrived at a full consensus with regard to all 'practical questions', but had realized that the Roman delegation had a totally different notion of 'tradition' and 'conformity'[1] in respect of doctrinal questions. Of course, both sides will have emphasized the transmission of Christian faith and the maintained identity of belief in ecclesiastical tradition. But when stating what these things might actually mean, both groups came to totally different conclusions. Rome justified the teaching of Vatican II on human religious freedom, which the Church, in agreement with previous tradition, had expressly rejected in the nineteenth century and at the beginning of the twentieth. This was Modernism raising its head again and was quite unacceptable to the Society of St Pius X. The same was true of ecumenical dialogue, which the Council of Trent had anathematized. Numerous traditionalist groups share the views of the Society in this regard. They generally reject Vatican II for those reasons and describe its defenders as 'old liberals'. This is the first type of speech block about Vatican II.

In November 2011, *Osservatore Romano* published Monsignor Ocariz's explanation of the response of the Roman delegation charged with negotiations. The teachings of Vatican II were defended by reference to the papal magisterium and the episcopal college assembled for the Council. Like all Councils in the past, Vatican II offered something new, yet this new aspect did not alter but deepened the faith. It was a question not of a 'hermeneutics of discontinuity', but of hermeneutics as revision.[2] Furthermore, the rules that had applied hitherto also applied to the individual teachings of Vatican II: only what was unambiguously defined as dogma called for an assent of faith *(assensus fidei)*. Teachings which were not defined as dogma, but were proffered by the Church's authentic magisterium, called for the religious assent *(assensus religiosus)* and religious obedience *(oboedientia religiosa)* of the faithful.

Bruno Gherardini, a professor of theology for many years at the papal Lateran University, former Dean of the faculty of theology there and a canon of St Peter's,[3] tells us that the texts of Vatican II on religious freedom and ecumenical dialogue are obviously not dogmatic definitions, for they are not texts of the infallible magisterium. But then Bishop Fellay's line of argument remains unanswered. Surely a tradition that reaches back several hundred years, and can invoke the definitions of the Council of Trent, is of greater theological weight with regard to ecumenical dialogue than the pronouncements of the authentic magisterium of the Fathers of Vatican II? Surely the same argument applies to religious freedom? The position which Monsignor Ocariz has put forward on the basis of the *Notificatio*[4] of Bishop Felici, General Secretary of the Council, clearly also results in a form of speech block about the Council, although in this case the mutism is of a different kind since it arises from an attempt to defend the Council.

The third reason for a spreading inability to say anything about the Council originates in the conciliar documents themselves. The source is *Gaudium et spes*, the pastoral constitution on the Church in the World. This constitution whole and entire was the work of the Council itself and encountered opposition from the very start. There were constant objections to it. Considerable uncertainties about the draft, which was finally accepted for discussion and revision in full assembly, were raised by theologians such as Karl Rahner, and by the German Bishops' Conference, de Lubac and European and non-European bishops. It was not clear how historically-contingent statements of principle could be binding. The socio-ethical basis of the Church's social teaching which had prevailed hitherto was to be replaced by theological propositions. But it was not clear how this might be done in a methodically respectable way. The uncertainty in this regard is obvious in Joseph Ratzinger's judgement, written in 1975 and republished in his *Theologische Prinzipienlehre* (Theological Principles) of 1982:[5] 'Whether the Council becomes a positive force in the history of the Church is only indirectly dependent on texts and committees. The decisive factor is whether there are individuals – saints – who achieve something new and vital by their own personal voluntary effort. Ultimately, the estimate of the historical value of Vatican II will depend on people's individual experience and endurance of the drama of the separation of the wheat and the chaff...'[6]

The uncertainty is no less apparent in the still contested interpretation of the exact meaning of 'signs of the times'. The speech block is evident in the insinuation that a misplaced optimistic belief in progress must have allowed the Fathers of the Council to be seduced into identifying theology with modern development. But this would mean that, seen as a whole, *Gaudium et spes* does not unfold the *ratio fidei* but the *ratio mundi huius*, asserting not the Christian faith but a justification of this world, even though the text of this constitution also contains a series of statements of faith. But what applies to *Gaudium et spes* in particular is simultaneously true of the Council and its teachings as a whole, though of course with certain changes in individual documents that do not affect the main issue. It is scarcely possible to understand the talk of a 'para-conciliar ideology' that has been spreading in references to Vatican II in any other way. It was proposed by Monsignor Pozzo, Secretary of the 'Ecclesia Dei' commission responsible for negotiations with the Society of St Pius X, during his initial address to members of the Society in Wigratzbad.[7]

II How can we start talking about the Council again?

The Fathers of Vatican II placed an 'Introduction: The situation of humankind in the world today' at the beginning of *Gaudium et spes*.[8] This prologue describes in all its tragic complications the new era in which people are living now, and the profound transformation of all the circumstances of life attributable to modern science, technology, the immense potential of increased power, and the 'spectre of a war of total destruction'. The introduction says of religious life: 'As regards religion there is a completely new atmosphere that conditions its practice. On the one hand, people are taking a hard look at all magical world-views and prevailing superstitions and demanding a more personal and active commitment of faith, so that not a few have achieved a lively sense of the divine. On the other hand, greater numbers are falling away from the practice of religion. In the past it was the exception to repudiate God and religion to the point of abandoning them, and then only in individual cases; but nowadays it seems a matter of course to reject them as incompatible with scientific progress and a new kind of humanism. In many places it is not only in philosophical terms that such trends are expressed, but there are signs of them in literature, art, the humanities, the interpretation of history and even civil law: all of which is very disturbing to many people.' (GS 7)

It is scarcely possible to describe the present religious situation of humanity more accurately. Is there any trace of a deceptively optimistic faith in progress affecting the conciliar Fathers? Not in this passage, at any rate.

The Fathers of the Council are addressing believing Christians and all human beings in this new context. They talk of revelation and the Church and of their relevance to human beings as they know they must talk in order not only to be true to the Gospel but for the sake of authenticity. They may not offer a pinpointed, up-to-date conceptual account of the epochal transformation that is taking place, but pastoral experience and care have certainly made them aware of how to talk about faith in the modern world. They have been able to clarify this sensitivity to the times by intensive discussions with one another, by consulting theologians, and by confrontation with the public opinion that surges through the media every day.

The general sense of the appropriateness of this approach that so vitally informed the Council also characterized and supported the first phase of its reception, covering approximately the first 20 years until the Roman Synod of 1985. These two decades saw a systematic engagement in dialogue with the Eastern Churches and with the Churches and ecclesial communities of the Reformation. Forms of interreligious dialogue, especially Christian–Jewish discussions, were initiated, and existing concordats with 'Catholic States' were revised to accommodate religious freedom; the new Code of Canon Law (*Codex Iuris Canonici*) of 1983 came into force; and – especially important – the liturgy was reformed. Then there were the diocesan and national synods, such as the Medellín Latin American Synod, which tried to apply the Council to various pastoral circumstances. At the same time, the bishops' conferences institutionalized the new consultative committees at parish and diocesan levels, the religious Orders and Congregations reformed their organizations, missionary work was restructured, and development work and efforts to promulgate human rights won their own specific place in the Church's procedures. Hitherto unknown modes of cooperation between different local churches and parishes or communities developed beyond the mere despatch of priests to parts of the world where they were scarce, already practised under Pius XII. The interpretative work to be done, the hermeneutics of the Council, was described at the 1985 Synod with the traditional specifications and conditions, and the particular character of the Council, its innovatory nature, was defined as '*communio*-ecclesiology'. The talk that seemed to have vanished was now far from absent, and many good things were achieved in and through it.

But there were intimations of future disputes. Talking and listening to one another became difficult, and speech blocks began to develop from confrontations. These undoubtedly included the promulgation of the encyclical *Humanae vitae* and ranged from moral theologians' abandonment of a traditional natural-law approach in favour of a differentiated citation of biological facts to an insistence on the primordial principle of the dignity of the individual and personal responsibility. There were also the contentious aspects of the theology of liberation, which invoked *Gaudium et spes*, and the associated criticism of church structures and the Roman reactions to them.

The next two decades of reception had three major aspects: an evolving scholarly examination of the complex of problems raised by the Council by means of historical research and theological interpretation; a continuation of interreligious and ecumenical dialogue, but with some signs of exhaustion; and increased polarizations within the Church. These confrontations went beyond work on the history of Vatican II and theological interpretations. They were not only directed against practical questions examined in the Council, such as the collegiality of bishops, the autonomy of local churches within the unity of the whole Church, the participation of local churches in the choice of their bishops, and new modes of procedure such as those expressed in ecumenical and interreligious dialogue. Questions were asked about new and large-scale problems, which had now come to the fore, such as the position of women in the Church, ecological questions, the conditions for entry to the priesthood, and whether the presuppositions of the Council called not for traditional but for new solutions.

A more comprehensive form of speechlessness started in this second phase of reception. It was not concerned with the personal witness to faith of John Paul II during his long sickness. This speech block had to do with the Church and its capability of regeneration and reform. This particular mutism has continued to spread since the beginning of Benedict XVI's pontificate. It is provoked not only by individual measures, such as the direct introduction of the 'extraordinary rite' without consultations and discussions with the bishops' conferences, the exceptional attention paid to the Society of St Pius X in spite of its severely polemical attitude, the anti-Semitism of Bishop Williamson, and so on. The faithful also note with something more than mere surprise the countless warning-signs which Pope Benedict and certain bishops use to announce their return to pre-conciliar usages and rules. Many committed believers who in the past took an active part in, for instance, synods or diocesan days of celebration are increasingly convinced that it is no longer possible to communicate with the hierarchy in the present phase of the post-conciliar Church. Any attempt at discussion they would say, has become pointless. Anything like that is a sheer waste of time. Essentially, it seems, the hierarchical Church is concerned solely to carry on in the old ways and to ensure self-preservation.

But when these three kinds of mutism prevail, the Word of God is no longer heard in the Church, and it is not the transcendental-pragmatic *apriori* in which God's Word is audible to human beings.

III A basic resource for understanding and overcoming this speech block

With the abovementioned modes of speechlessness we encounter a phenomenon which modern universal linguistic pragmatics enables us to elucidate to a certain extent. Since Wittgenstein, the most varied scientific theories accept the notion that both the natural sciences and the humanities are essentially dependent on linguistic mediation. In the empirical sciences, the material object of the science in question is not observation but perception as mediated by language. This linguistic mediation of scientific perception and observation comprises verification, falsification, the protocols of the observer and the discourse of the scientific community. The same is true of the human sciences. Basically, a distinction is to be made between the utterance and that which is uttered. Yet, what is uttered is always given and disclosed only in the utterance, though it is never totally subsumed in it.

Modern linguistic analysis has also come to distinguish between semantics, grammar and pragmatics. Pragmatics investigates the use of language by the speaker and the hearer, who must participate in the actual use of language in order to understand it. Rules apply here. Anyone who, say, wants to tell the truth about this or that matter necessarily and factually suggests that the universal validity of the truth of the matter in question will be evident in the discourse now under way. In other words: 'The basic rules of communicative behaviour aimed at understanding include recognition of the intentionality of the process of understanding in the sense of a mutual and reciprocal we-understanding as well as the intention to understand with regard to the thematic object, and finally the self-acknowledged intentionality of this overall process of intending the process of understanding.'[9] In the empirical world, we encounter *a priori* aspects which result from the freedom of the will and are non-derivable from and non-attributable to anything else. In general, we learn how transcendental thinking has become more profound and has been universalized beyond the Kantian procedure.

What can the insights of modern linguistic philosophy that I have outlined tell us about the abovementioned types of speech block? As an initial approach, we might attempt a formal representation of the linguistic situation of Bishop Fellay and Monsignor Ocariz talking about faith:

Fellay says: Vatican II teaches that Christian faith is compatible with religious freedom and ecumenical dialogue. According to pronouncements of the magisterium (the *Syllabus of Errors* and the rejection of Modernism; the Council of Trent), the Christian faith is not compatible with religious freedom and ecumenical dialogue. Therefore Vatican II alters the identity of faith.
Ocariz says: According to magisterial pronouncements of Vatican II, religious freedom and ecumenical dialogue are compatible with the Christian faith. The identity of faith is maintained in spite of the earlier magisterial pronouncements cited.

The definition of the authority of the magisterium is the same on both sides. The conclusions are contradictory.[10] If a will to truth is ascribed to both sides, then the truth compels both sides to seek agreement with regard to the identity of faith.[11] The identity of faith is an unconditional identity pure and simple, since faith believes in God who reveals himself, the creative Word of God himself, and does so precisely on the basis of God's authority. This Word of God has been revealed in Jesus Christ, in his message, his passion and his cross, in his elevation to the Father, and in the sending of his Spirit. All the faithful bear witness to the identity of this divine faith, and it is essentially in human language that the apostles and their successors proclaim and present it with binding effect. Faith is uttered and testified to in this human discourse, but faith is not exhaustively subsumed in the words of that discourse. Bearing witness to faith means that faith is enunciated on the presupposition that the language used is uttered in a pragmatic context appropriate to faith.

Yet, this means in essence that the identity of faith cannot be straightforwardly equated with the identity of the language of the magisterium considered as terms pure and simple, which is possible only insofar as those terms are credible, though always era-specific, expressions[12] for the identity of faith. New insights of linguistic philosophy and the associated semiotic pragmatics of recent origin enable us to see why the traditional dogmatic theology of principles[13] did not pose the question of historicity and temporality, and of the historical nature of the conceptual forms taken by the language of belief and dogmatic theology, on the one hand, and the question of the identity of belief, on the other, as they have to be posed today for the very sake of the identity of faith.

IV The language of faith and the historical approach implied throughout the texts of Vatican II

The abovementioned considerations with regard to the discussions between Bishop Fellay and Monsignor Ocariz will help us to understand the actual nature of the language of faith, and the modern way of thinking in the texts of Vatican II as a whole, implied in that language. The major constitutions will serve as a basis: *Dei verbum*, the dogmatic constitution on divine revelation; *Lumen gentium*, the dogmatic constitution on the Church; *Gaudium et spes*, the pastoral constitution on the Church in the modern world; and *Sacrosanctum concilium*, the constitution on the sacred liturgy, though in the last-mentioned case only the first chapter, which is constitutional, is relevant, since the other sections contain individual principles of reform and practical suggestions for their implementation.

A preliminary observation is that the constitution *Dei verbum* begins with the words: 'Hearing the Word of God with reverence...' (DV 1). The holy

Synod itself hears the Word of God, through whom God made everything (DV 3), through whom God himself of his loving kindness reveals himself to humankind (DV 2), 'and the works performed by God in the history of salvation show forth and bear out the doctrine and realities signified by the words'. This Word was made flesh in Jesus Christ (DV 2). By his passion and his resurrection from the dead, and by sending the Spirit of truth, 'he completed and perfected Revelation and confirmed it with divine guarantees' (DV 4). Accordingly, it is a divine Revelation, the one Word of God himself, that is shown forth in the whole sacred economy, preparing the way in the most varied events and in the words of the prophets, and finally by the presence and self-manifestation of Jesus Christ. This Word of God is heard by the Church today, and has been heard by the Fathers of the Council. There is a clear difference between these pronouncements and those of the Council of Trent and of Vatican I.[14] Using their specialized terminology, certain theologians would describe this as a 'breakthrough from an understanding of revelation based on instruction theory to one based on communication theory'. Vatican II's pronouncement on the revelation or self-disclosure of God in creation and history is made possible by its mediation through human words and human means of communication, in which it is enunciated without being subsumed purely and simply in and as the words themselves. Jesus' words receive assent as the Word of God only when they are accepted *in faith*. God's revelation, his Word, is not understood and affirmed in the perspective of being-in-the-world, that is, of the understanding of being, but only in the Holy Spirit himself. We are concerned here with the ancient question of understanding why there is anything at all and not nothing. It is an understanding of faith, for in their lives humans are first and foremost pilgrims on their way into the depths of the Word, and this pilgrimage reaches its bourne only in death. Accordingly the Word is a Word addressed to humankind out of unimaginable freedom, in and through creation, in and through history, and in and through Jesus Christ. It is a Word which allows the faithful to utter their totally heartfelt, unconditionally free assent to it. Because the Word of God is a word that can be answered and announced only in human words, it does not empower humanity to conceive of a universal historical system in the manner of Hegel.

Lumen gentium, the dogmatic constitution on the Church (which clearly takes the content of *Dei verbum* as read), begins with the mystery of revelation in Jesus Christ by means of which, from the beginning, God calls humanity to faith and therefore into his Church: that is, into community with him. 'Already present in figure at the beginning of the world, this Church was prepared in marvellous fashion in the history of the people of Israel and in the old Alliance. Established in this last age of the world, and made manifest in the outpouring of the Spirit, it will be brought to glorious completion at the end of time' (LG 2). Accordingly, the Church as mystery includes the entire history of salvation. It is an eschatological entity which is present in historical figures and forms yet is never absorbed and wholly consummated in them. It *subsists* in them. It does so in one way in the primordial alliance of Noah (*Nostra aetate* translates this as the 'truth' that prevails in religions and is recognized by the Church), in another way in the Old Testament people of the Covenant, and in yet another way in the Church; yet it is always the one Church of Jesus Christ, the Church as mystery. In each actual finite instance, God's revelation in Jesus Christ, and the inclusion in God's community that occurs in faith and in baptism, are presented and manifest in a form of communication which exceeds the bounds of each manifestation. The result is not an inclusive reconstruction of human community, because the forms in which faith can be expressed and fulfilled are always time-bound linguistic modes of communication. But they are also ways of communicating infused with faith, hope and love in which God's anticipatory loving-kindness is made manifest.

Gaudium et spes also proceeds on the basis of a mystery: the mystery of the human being, which is that Jesus Christ, the Word of God become flesh, has united himself with humanity (GS 22). 'As an innocent lamb he merited life for us by his blood which he freely shed. In him God reconciled us to himself and to one another, freeing us from the bondage of the devil and of sin...Conformed to the image of the Son who is the firstborn of many brothers, Christians receive the "first fruits of the Spirit" (Rom. 8.23), by which they are able to fulfil the new law of love. By this Spirit...the whole human is inwardly renewed, right up to the "redemption of the body" (Rom. 8.23)' (GS 22).

People discover by their own efforts that they are capable of good *and* evil. 'When they look into their own hearts they find they find that they are drawn towards what is wrong and sunk in many evils'. In fact: 'Humans are divided in themselves' (the human person is '*in se ipso divisus*', GS 13). Human beings are not identical with themselves if in the course of achieving freedom they fail to keep their freedom in proper bounds. Humans have in their hearts a law inscribed by God and their 'intellectual nature finds at last its perfection...in wisdom, which gently draws the human mind to look for what is true and good'. The bounds of their freedom are shown in the dignity of the intellect (GS 15), in the dignity of moral conscience (GS 16), and in the dignity of freedom itself. 'Human dignity requires people to act out of conscious and free choice, as moved and drawn in a personal way from within, and not by blind impulses in themselves or by mere external constraint' (GS 17). People realize freedom in authentic liberty only when they recognize the fundamental and unconditional nature of the essential equality and equal dignity of all human beings (GS 29). Here the Fathers of the Council refer to the modern principle of self-determination and the autonomy of freedom as formulated by Kant, but present it in its fully-realized form as faith in Jesus Christ. Because empirical human freedom is characterized by unconditional human dignity, it so to speak prefigures perfect transcendental freedom. It is at this point precisely that believers finds the infinitely loving and affirmative God in the freedom revealed in Jesus Christ's perfect devotion to humanity derived from his unity with the Father and conveyed through his Spirit. But this communication of believers fulfilling their freedom must still take place in faith and hope in the Holy Spirit who has been given to them, for only the experience of death enables human beings actually to overcome their most radical non-identity.[15]

This freedom emerges from the presence of transcendental unconditionalities in the empirical sphere on which the very empiricism of the empirical is wholly dependent. The same is true of those fundamental phenomena which, according to Heidegger, as they show themselves (*phainesthai* = manifestation and semblance), make possible the multiplicity of phenomena. The modern faith-language of Vatican II implies these modes of thinking about the subject, yet its conjunction of principles and empirical data would seem to be methodically impermissible. But a proficient interpretation can banish this apparent inconsistency, and we have a cure for the third kind of speech block. By now it should be clear why I described the Church as a theological *apriori* of faith. It is so because it offers the pre-given pragmatics that enables Christians to fulfil their faith in the threefold God who reveals himself to them.

Translated by J. G. Cumming

Notes

1. Cf. Bishop Fellay's sermon on relations with Rome, www.piusbruderschaft.de/archiv-news/734-beziehungen (20 February 2012).
2. Cf. www.osservatoreromano.va/portal/dt?JSPT TabContaine... (21 February 2012).
3. Cf. Brunero Gherardini, *Chiesa–Tradizione–Magistero*, under: www.chiesaepost concilio.blogspot.com/20111/12/ons-brunero... (21 February 2012).
4. Cf. Peter Hünermann, 'Die Dokumente des Zweiten Vatikanischen Konzils', in *Herders Theologischer Kommentar zum Zweiten Vatikanischen Konzil* (HthKVat. II), vol. 1, Freiburg im Breisgau, 2004, pp. 186f: 'With regard to conciliar usage and the pastoral objectives of the present Council, this Holy Synod defines only those aspects of faith and morals as to be adhered to as of the Church which it has itself declared to be such. But all believing Christians must receive and understand the rest of what the Holy Synod proposes as the teaching of the highest magisterium of the Church in conformity to the intention of the Holy Synod itself, which will be evident either from the constitutive object or mode of the pronouncement, in accordance with the rules of theological exposition.'
5. Joseph Ratzinger, 'Der Weltdienst der Kirche. Auswirkungen von *Gaudium et spes* im letzten Jahrzehnt', in Andreas Bunch, Alfred Gläser & Michael Seybold (eds), *Zehn Jahre Vaticanum II*, Regensburg,1976; Joseph Ratzinger, *Theologische Prinzipienlehre. Bausteine zur Fundamentaltheologie*, Munich, 1982, pp. 390–409.
6. Joseph Ratzinger, *Theologische Prinzipienlehre, op. cit.*, pp. 394f.
7. Cf. FSSP (Priesterbruderschaft Sankt Petrus = St Peter's Priests' Association), address by Monsignor Guido Pozzo in Wigratzbad on 2 July 2010, www.fssp.org/de/pozzo2010.htm (26.3.2011).
8. *Gaudium et Spes* 4—11.
9. Eberhard Simons, 'Transzendentalphilosophie und Sprachpragmatik', in Hans Michael Baumgartner (ed.), *Prinzip Freiheit–Eine Auseinandersetzung um Chancen und Grenzen Transzendentalphilosophischen Denkens* (*Praktische Philosophie*, vol. 10), Freiburg im Breisgau & Munich, 1979, p. 51.
10. Pope John Paul II's statement on the condemnation of Archbishop Lefebvre mentioned Lefebvre's denial of 'living tradition'. This was a metaphorical reference to a 'time factor' that had to be taken into consideration, but there was no theological elucidation of the term. It does not appear in Monsignor Ocariz's statement.
11. Cf. the abovementioned basic rule of linguistic pragmatics.
12. This 'era-specific credibility' of 'terms' is evident in the arguments for religious freedom and in the justifications for ecumenical dialogue to be found in *Dignitatis humanae* and *Unitatis redintegratio*.
13. It originated in the modern period. In his presentation of *loci theologici*, Melchior Cano does not mention the complex of theological problems essentially associated with human language, whereas Thomas Aquinas expressly discusses the restriction of human language in respect of divine matters.
14. Cf. DH 1501–1508; 3004–3007.
15. For a more detailed account, see Hermann Krings, 'Reale Freiheit. Praktische Freiheit. Transzendentale Freiheit', in: *id.*, *System und Freiheit*, Munich, 1980, pp. 40–68; also *id.*, 'Freiheit. Ein Versuch Gott zu denken', in *ibid.*, pp. 161–84.

Roncalli and 'his' Council

ALBERTO MELLONI

Angelo Giuseppe Roncalli, class of 1881, the first 'Italian' pope of a unified Italy, native of lands visited by St Charles (Borromeo) 300 years earlier, was a perfect product of what the Council of Trent dreamed of as a reformed and reforming priest and bishop. He had no reverential complex about that *segment* of tradition, which others still thought of as *the* tradition, and he had none of the gnawing anxiety that drove the intellectual progress of Congar, Rahner, Chenu and other great theologians of Vatican II.

I Homo Tridentinus?

His own way gave him access to a culture that connected him with everything which others found that culture obstructed. Roncalli loved being a priest and being a bishop, with an anti-careerist rigour and absolute moral purity. For this priest and this bishop, making the Tridentine dream come true meant completing it, making it real in a new way and a new *form*. He did it for historical reasons inherent in that Council, its conditions, its agenda. These were all things that the Tridentine priest felt with absolute immediacy and simplicity. Free from the complex which saw the fight with modernity as only way of defending the rigour of truth, Roncalli explored a radical trust in *the human as it is,* because *the human as it is* is what seeks redemption and already expresses that in its own historical signs.[1]

This is how Roncalli felt the word of the Gospel, the wisdom of Thomas à Kempis, the rhetoric of preachers, the allegories of the Fathers, descriptions of the ceremonial of consecration. What might seem fragmented and extrinsic to most people belonged for him to a complex of authoritative guidelines to follow faithfully; in spite of the papacy, it could be said, since when he became pope he assumed the functions of the bishop of Rome in a direct way. Once again, he did so without proclaiming any rupture and without anyone feeling it expressly as a rupture. But in his enjoyment of celebrating with the people, his visits to parish churches, his conversations with his own clergy, Roncalli expressed himself as a perfect Tridentine bishop, though shuffling the cards (unchanged for centuries) of a hierarchology that would consider defining the pope as bishop of Rome to be little less than an form of offensive reductionism.

Not only that. The Tridentine Roncalli knew that the measure of his task was not an abstract job description, but the principle of *salus animarum* and, whether in Bulgaria, Turkey, Greece, France and then explosively in Venice, his preaching style, *precipuus episcoporum munus,* was an object of continual attention. In Rome, this priest (without privileged access to modern exegesis, let alone to pastoralism *à la page*) became the instrument by which the faithful who heard him understood his ultimate intentions. A 1960 photograph at the Lenten station of St Sabina perfectly demonstrates the spontaneous *response* of the Roman people to this man, who did not scorn a bishop's ministry: 'Long live the Bishop of Rome!' proclaims a big banner in the large block capitals of a cycling-race fan or a trade-union demonstration. This has enormous ecclesiological relevance, for John XXIII certainly accepted that definition, not as a limitation of universal power, but as its foundation on the fatherly and brotherly relationship expressed in his greeting to the faithful on the night of 11 October 1962.

II The sprouting of the Council

In this awareness and without any apprenticeship, John XXIII could say that he had felt 'the word "council" *sprouting*' from his lips on 25 January 1959, less than 100 days after his election to the see of Peter. Roncalli, a priest of the generation that expected a council at any time, announced *his* council just like that. Having acquired some idea of how the curia thought and worked, and having gathered at the conclave that this choice was expected of him, he sought the opinion of the Secretary of State, whom he himself called Domenico Tardini [Slowcoach].[2] He announced the Council, together with all the 'buts' that had been put forward to him. There was to be a council, yes, *but* the codex would need to be reformed first; a council yes, *but* a synod for Rome would be necessary. He announced it with the feelings of someone who knew that, 'seventeen years after the end of World War II', it was time to heal the *scars*[3] of the two wars that had brought an era to a close and opened a new one, in which the Tridentine priest stood, without fear and without pessimistic illusions about what awaited the world. He said as much when he proclaimed the doctrine of mercy in the opening speech of the Council, which I think is worth re-reading simply because of the space it gives to a non-spiritualistic vision of the faith.[4] An 'off-air' remark captured by the RAI (*Radiotelevisione italiana*: Italian state broadcasting company) microphones, documents Roncalli's reaction to what was being said about him: 'Someone says, I've heard it myself, that the Pope is too optimistic, that he only sees the good, that he sees everything from that angle, the good. But, of course. I cannot separate myself (in my own way, naturally) from our Lord, who did nothing but pour out good around him, happiness, peace and encouragement'.[5]

Following the example of Jesus 'in my own way', as he had understood from 1903, according to his *Journal of a Soul*, was the fairly unoriginal novelty that Roncalli brought and brought to the papacy as a Christian: a Christian who had the chance to summon a council and did summon one, who felt that it was his duty to give expression to all the demands of the Church and did 'express' them, who had the power to open and clearly did 'open' a council that could be described as new because of its 'pastoral' character.

III Gaudet

Certainly, for Roncalli, Vatican II was *like that*. It was pastoral, and could not be otherwise than *like that*. He said this in *Gaudet Mater Ecclesia,* his opening Vatican II address on 11 October 1962, which was incomprehensible to those seeking a conciliar programme, or the specific opportunity for renewal that the Council brought with it.

For Roncalli, there was a form of the magisterium that Vatican II had adapt to: the pastoral mode. This was not because it concerned itself with parochial minutiae, but because it told the truth in a way consistent with the saving and merciful nature of the person of Jesus. Such a stringent and simple criterion was inaccessible and incomprehensible to many, then and later. In its light, all the categorizations invented for the purpose of boiling Vatican II in a soup of trivia and trimmings wilted away.

The 'doctrinal' council, which in the pecking order of academic theology should stand at the top of any classification of councils, was (according to the man who should be considered 'the' father of Vatican II) something that had no reason to be *here and now*. There was no need for a council to repeat doctrine that everyone already knew, in which theological reception processes and historical settling processes had *already* distinguished between the unrelinquishable and the ephemeral, the ideological and the necessary, and separated what was alive from what was useless; or, to put it in a Congarian way, the system from the truth.[6] The point under discussion was how to restore its *own* eloquence to the Gospel. As Roncalli, the *homo Tridentinus*, defined it in *Gaudet Mater Ecclesia*, this was a matter of 'reclothing it', because the Gospel wears clothes and only undresses after it has been communicated, never before.

Roncalli's vision was one of Christian truth and the need for its intimate communication, which does not need great renewals of a systematic kind or dramatic gestures to express itself. So Roncalli retained not a 'leftover' but what was his own: his enjoyment and satisfaction at being a Christian who remained one, while the scenery of the twentieth century passed behind, within and over him, without ever succeeding in scratching his substantial theological opening to the human.

IV The human

In the end, this was what Roncalli's Christianity came down to: a firm position, yet so transparent that it lent itself to many crude simplifications. For Roncalli, the human had nothing to do with the 'anthropological turning point' of theology in the 1960s, or with its pastoral or even politicized sub-products of the end of the twentieth century. A reader of the Greek Fathers in an improbable meeting with the Catholic ambassadors in the East,[7] Roncalli did not even use the category of *theosis* (deification), in the sense of the human eschatological destiny which also illuminates particular experience. Not that he ever shared that late nineteenth-century moral sensibility, which considered the human as a corpse for autoptic exercises intended to educate the confessor who (because of this?) was unemployed by the end of the following century. And, of course, Roncalli did not share either of the two visions which, from the Council onwards, confronted (and even came into conflict with) each other, and which Joseph Komonchak has rightly described as one of the hermeneutical keys to Vatican II and its reception.[8]

Roncalli did not belong to the large, bipartite cultural family of Thomists. They were capable of holding very diverse opinions, ranging from the most ardently reformist to the most obstinately conservative. John

XXIII did not take offence at Leonine neo-Thomism, or even at the return to scholasticism for anti-Modernist purposes. His Thomas was merely a few formulae, short theses, and never reading matter.

However, Roncalli was even less aligned with the other decisive group at Vatican II, the Augustinians. They were the ones who quite often began their course of very radical or even subversive positions with an affirmation a good deal stronger than their affirmation of the Church. But it is precisely from *this* spiritual rather than theological sensibility that the strongest second thoughts arose about the complexity of the Council's development and its reception. A radical pessimism about the wound of sin, and lack of respect for the human creature, in whom, as well as the invisible finger of God, the pride of the individual can be seen at work, led them to consider any attempt at reform to be futile and bankrupt. They had scant respect for that inner dynamism which alone would guarantee genuine progress. Precisely because it was elusive, they thought it should be put in brackets and replaced by a passive maintenance of the *status quo*. Such things were completely alien to Pope John, who moved on a different plane altogether.

The two world wars had put him in contact with the victims in a way that interacted unexpectedly with his faith. The hundreds of children flitting about behind the war front when he passed through the 'Guerrone',[9] the sound of the Stalin revolution clearly audible from the Bulgaria of the first decade after Lenin's death,[10] contact with the Shoah on the shores of the Bosphorus, where the most dramatic accounts and documents on the extermination of the Jews were arriving like previews from agents of the Jewish agency,[11] assistance directed towards the rebirth of French democracy and the formation of new bodies for multi-lateral diplomacy,[12] all made him look with new eyes on the successive efforts to regulate conflicts and build peace and détente.

Of course these efforts quite often evoked Roncallian expressions that approach the suspicion and even aversion of the prevailing magisterium. But when these efforts became expressions by particular people, and he had to exercise direct responsibility over them, then we find him unexpectedly giving credit, trust and solidarity. This might happen with the Orthodox Bulgarians or with the Zionists resident in Istanbul, with the deputies of the French MRP [*Mouvement Républicain Populaire* = Popular Republican Movement] or with Fanfaniani young people in Venice, who favoured an openness towards the left (he kept his distance from them but spread a protective cloak over them because of the hardships he saw besetting these 'good little children').[13] Or else it might happen because of a generosity of treatment which the interlocutor understood very well, and which Roncalli usually noted in the diary with evasive formulae (such as 'we understood each other well'), when, effectively, the contents have nearly always been evaded..

The way in which Roncalli interpreted this openness to the human as a key to the universality demanded by the papal function did not refer in isolation to the function of pastor of the universal Church, but to the fatherhood and the *munus* of bishop which unite both roles. Thus, John XXIII felt himself to be called to an effort to understand everybody, so that the distinction between the sin and the sinner (a quotation from St Augustine that had remained dormant for centuries)[14] acquired its own dynamism in view of the Council and within the Council. Precisely as a liturgical encounter with the face of Christ, the Council had the task of making peace, not with modernity, as the syllabus feared, but with humanity in search of peace.

V The beginning

Naturally, such a prospect brought conflicts: conflicts up till then suppressed by churchmen of a type that that Giuseppe de Luca described, in an eloquent metaphor, to Giovanni Battista Montini, who knew them well, as vultures flapping round the ancient head of the Church: 'The Rome that you know and from which you were exiled does not show signs of changing, as it seemed would happen in the end. After its first fright, the circle of old vultures returns. Slowly. But it does return. And it returns with a lust for new torments, new vendettas. Around the *carum caput* [i.e. Pope John] that macabre circle presses. Certainly it has regrouped.'[15]

Precisely because this was his apparent destiny, Roncalli's effort now deserves a rigorous study. It is not just an academic point that this transition signalled a new beginning (like Chalcedon, for which Karl Rahner minted the phrase): something that brought an end to an era, according to a dynamic well-known to historical critical research. With Roncalli a period came to an end, not because a historical project had been accomplished, and not by the success of a cunning plan by a counter-power. That was the mantra of a disparaging propaganda which considered the election of 'Nikita Roncalli' to be the victory of who knows what diabolical machinations.[16]

A careful study of the sources shows just the opposite, and how Roncalli came from that very world whose updating he called for. He lived through the anti-Modernist crisis as a seminarian and as a priest. He was a diplomat of the Vatican diplomacy of Ratti and Pacelli.[17] He became Patriarch of Venice in the course of an ecclesiastical career. He ascended the papal throne in a completely normal conclave at which consensus and good will were called for. The point of difference was not in the project (there was none) but in certain fundamental elements of his spirituality and of his culture, the way he lived, which he also allowed to speak for the institutional roles he played. Roncalli was elected at the conclave because he had a deserved reputation for being a prudent and peaceful man. But the break was not just in the choice of a man known to be pious. The break came because he believed he must 'play' pope by giving power and room to govern to a spiritual attitude that permeated him.[18] He carved it out (I think that is the way to put it) from his reading and from Scripture. In short, there are elements of his culture that he first adopted, then cultivated and finally set to work in his government. These made it possible for the Church to adopt a new position towards history, and towards the Lord of both.[19]

These are the living nerves of what in his 'conciliar' Council was called *aggiornamento*.[20] But if we want to know *how* Roncalli upset an institutional and ecclesiastical balance, which would have kept the riches of Catholicism locked up for times still to come, we find the contradiction between a Tridentine priest, quite at home in the forms and devotions of that period, yet capable of choosing and returning towards the sources of a tradition less compromised by a closed confessionality, by the *philautia* [self-love] of the anti-modern. For Roncalli, that choice, which on the historical level amounts to a break, was an obedience.

VI Vitality

For Catholicism at the end of the 1950s the accession to power of this obedience represented an injection of vitality. The problem of mid-twentieth-century Catholicism was not the choice between rigour and laxity, between the defence of truth and the betrayal of truth. That false dichotomy was one that an obsolete cultural model (*fin-de-siècle* intransigence and the Roman schools) circulated to back a call for immobility, for a submission which was a cover-up for laziness. The choice was one between sham and substance, between system and truth (as Congar put it),[21] between bureaucratic power and trusting in the life-giving poverty of gospel simplicity.

It is in this obedience that we can set John XXIII's choice to 'play pope' in a neglected area of the magisterium. The nineteenth- and twentieth-century papacy had chosen to emphasize the magisterium, but also to reduce its scope drastically. As I have noted, during the nineteenth century, the term 'magisterium', embracing all the teaching in its complex variety, became restricted to the doctrinal exercise of church authority, especially that of the pope as custodian and source of the ordinary magisterium. This tended to absorb historical-theological work and reduce it to commentary, passing from one papal act to another.[22] In fact, that tendency (for which there are authoritative surviving testimonies) had a grim effect on the way bishops functioned, as they were forced into perpetual haemorrhagic repetition of their fidelity to papal teaching.[23] Bishops were forced to emulate a model of authority which spread the cover of doctrine over ever greater areas (private morality, social doctrine and so forth), and left increasingly little space for vital dimensions of Christian life, such as meditating on the scriptures, spirituality or prayer.

With the Council, John XXIII marked a break with that scenario, because the consensus he gathered round his person was not entirely determined by such processes,[24] but was based on the recognition of a role–that of spiritual master–which the bishops of Rome had forgotten to play. The new horizon he tried to open up for the Council was that which had sealed the substance of the Christian profession and the function of bishop.[25] It remained a horizon that was wholly Christian.

Translated by Dinah Livingstone

Notes

1. M.-D. Chenu, *Parole de Dieu, I: La foi dans l'intelligence; II: L'évangile dans le temps*, Paris, 1964.
2. On those who gradually made suggestions, and for an account of the dialogue between the Pope and the head of a curia accustomed to 'ponder', as John XXIII called it, cf. A. Melloni, *Papa Giovanni. Un cristiano e il suo concilio*, Turin, 2009, p. 212.
3. Cf the radio message of 11/9/1962, *Discorsi, Messaggi, Colloqui del S. P. Giovanni XXIII*, Vatican City, vol. IV, 1959–1965, pp. 524–5.
4. Cf. Melloni, *Papa Giovanni, op. cit.*, which gives the critical edition of the variants.
5. Clip of 31 March 1962, found by F. Nardelli and F. Ruozzi in the Teche RAI, now in A. Melloni-F. Nardelli-F. Ruozzi, *Pacem in terris, un documentario videostorico*, Bologna, 2008.
6. Cf. my 'The System and the Truth in the Diaries of Yves Congar', in *Yves Congar Theologian of the Church*, G. Flynn (ed.), Louvain, Paris & Dudley, 2005, pp. 277–302.

7. Cf. memoirs of Ambassador P. Poswick, *Un journal du concile. Vatican II vu par un diplomate belge*, Paris, 2005, and the testimony of his son Ferdinand. See below.
8. J.A. Komonchak, 'Le valutazioni sulla Gaudium et spes', in *Chi ha paura del concilio? Studi sull'ermeneutica del Vaticano II*, essays by P. Hünermann, J. Komonchak, A. Melloni, G. Ruggieri & C. Theobald, Rome, 2009, pp. 115–25.
9. R. Morozzo della Rocca, *La fede e la guerra. Cappellani militari e preti-soldati (1915–1919)*, Rome, 1980.
10. F. Della Salda, *Obbedienza e pace. La missione del vescovo A .G. Roncalli in Bulgaria (1925–1934)*, Genoa, 1988.
11. D. Porat, '"He read in tears the documents which I requested him to transmit to his Patron in Rome" – A Wartime Triangle: Pope Pius XII, Monsignor Angelo G. Roncalli and a Jewish Delegate in Istanbul', *Cristianesimo nella storia*, XXVII (2006), pp. 599–632.
12. C. F. Casula & A. Liliosa, *Unesco 1945–2005: una utopia necessaria. Scienza, cultura educazione nel secolo mondo*, Troina, 2005.
13. Cf. E. Galavotti, *Introduzione a A. G. Roncalli – Giovanni XXIII, Pace e Vangelo. Agende del patriarca*, vol. 1: 1953–1955, Bologna, 2008.
14. G. Alberigo, 'Dal bastone alla misericordia. Il magistero nel cattolicesimo contemporaneo (1830–1980)', *Cristianesimo nella storia*, II (1981), pp. 487–521.
15. Letter of 6 August 1959, G. De Luca & G.B. Montini, *Carteggio 1930–1962*, edited by P. Vian, *Studium*, Rome, 1992, p. 232; on the author R. Guarnieri, *Don Giuseppe De Luca, Tra cronaca e storia*, Cinisello Balsamo, 1991.
16. For a synthesis of the traditionalist positions, cf. R. Amerio, *Iota unum. Studio delle variazioni della Chiesa cattolica nel secolo XX*, Milan & Naples, 1985, pp. 42–78. Typical of the disparaging propaganda is: F. Bellegrandi, *Nikita Roncalli. Controvita di un papa*, Rome, 1995.
17. F. Della Salda, *Obbedienza e pace*, op. cit & A. Melloni, *Tra Istanbul, Atene e la guerra. A. G. Roncalli vicario e delegato apostolico (1935–1944)*, passim.
18. G. Lercaro, 'Linee per una ricerca su Giovanni XXIII', in *Per la forza dello Spirito*, Bologna, 1984, pp. 290–1.
19. On the formation of Roncalli's culture, cf.. Melloni, *Papa Giovanni*, op. cit., pp. 49–79.
20. G. Alberigo, 'L'amore alla Chiesa: dalla riforma all'aggiornamento', in *Con tutte le tue forze. I nodi della fede cristiana oggi. Omaggio a Giuseppe Dossetti*, A. & G. Alberigo (eds), Genoa, 1993, pp. 169–94.
21. A. Melloni, *The System and the Truth in the Diaries of Yves Congar*, op. cit., pp. 277–302.
22. Cf. Y. Congar, 'A Brief History of the Forms of the Magisterium and its Relations with Scholars', in *Readings in Moral Theology: The Magisterium and Morality*, Charles E. Curran & Richard A. McCormick (eds), New York, 1982, pp. 321–8; on more recent developments and the theological implications of the discussion, cf. G. Ruggieri, *La verità crocifissa. Il pensiero cristiano di fronte all'alterità*, Rome, 2007; contributions in *Cristianesimo nella storia*, XXI (2000), pp. 171–205; and G. Miccoli, *In difesa della fede. La chiesa di Giovanni Paolo II e Benedetto XVI*, Milan, 2007.
23. Lorenzo Milani described it with sharp and painful acumen in a letter to Pistelli in 1953, *Quel muro di foglio e d'incenso*, now in *Lettere di L. Milani*, M. Gesualdi (ed.), Cinisello Balsamo, 2007, pp. 142–55.
24. 'Papa Giovanni XXIII nel giudizio del mondo', *Herder-Korrespondenz* (1963).
25. G. Alberigo, 'L'ispirazione di un concilio ecumenico: le esperienze del Cardinale Roncalli', in *Le deuxième concile du Vatican (1959–1965)*, Rome, 1989, pp. 81–99.

Vatican II as Church Enacted

GIUSEPPE RUGGIERI

I What was the Second Vatican Council?

Generally, when we talk about Vatican II we ask about its teachings: what did the Council say about the Church, about the liturgy, about religious freedom, about the Jews, about non-Christian religions? These are legitimate questions, just as it is legitimate to ask what the Council of Trent taught about the mass as a sacrifice, what the Council of Chalcedon taught about the unity of Christ as God and man.

Often, however, we don't realize that another question is even more important and of a sort that makes a difference to our answer. The more important question is: what sort of council was Vatican II? No council has ever really been the same as another. Even the composition of the participants makes this true: just bishops, or laypeople as well or monks as well or theologians as well? We need only think of the role of the emperors in the councils of the first millennium, and also in some medieval councils such as Constance. And what churches were present through their bishops? On this point, Karl Rahner, in a famous lecture in 1979, commented that Vatican II was the first council of the universal Church in the history of Christianity. For the first time, the main actor at the Council was a body of bishops drawn from the whole world and not just a group of European bishops exported round the world in the form of European missionary bishops. This simple fact makes Vatican II different from Vatican I, whose concerns centred on the challenges to the European Catholic Church from developments in European societies.

And there is even now no understanding of what is meant by a 'pastoral' council, or one devoted to *aggiornamento*, and these terms are understood in a very crude sense, as a practical adaptation of the Church's doctrine – and this is in fact how they are understood by those who consider Vatican II an 'inferior' council to the 'dogmatic' councils of the past. There is no understanding even of the teaching, let alone the doctrinal change the Council introduced into the life of the Church. Pope John XXIII, in his opening address, said that the problem of the Council was not this or that article of doctrine, but a leap forward for 'doctrinal penetration and a formation of consciences', since a magisterium that is primarily pastoral in nature should be able to distinguish between the living substance of the Gospel and its clothing. The bishops in council took a whole week, one of the tensest of the Council (14–21 November 1962), to discuss the meaning of these words. And it was those (belonging to the minority hostile to the conciliar *aggiornamento*) who rejected, and continue to reject, this conception of doctrine: they argue that doctrine consists of principles and the pastoral element is the application of principles independent of history. But the majority of the bishops slowly understood this new approach to doctrine, which consists above all in the reinterpretation of the living substance of the Gospel in the language required by the history of men and women today, going beyond the classical dichotomy expressed in the 'formula *fides et mores* that had been dominant in late medieval and modern times, leaving behind the sectorialism, the abstractions and the legalism that this had underpinned'.[1]

Vatican II thus represented the venture of a whole Church concentrated on understanding the Gospel at its own moment in history. As Christoph Theobald emphasizes, it was a great act of 'tradition' in which the whole Church places itself in a position to listen to the living Word of the Gospel.[2] We can say the same thing in different words: the Council was the 'representation' of the Church 'enacted'.

II Representation of the Church

The category of *repraesentatio*/representation forms the spinal cord linking liturgy, Trinitarian theology, Christology, ecclesiology, and the very definition of Christian witness, especially in real and true martyrdom. Its restriction, from the sixteenth century, to the sphere of worship and ministry, did serious damage. The people who really took over the idea in modern times were the politicians, but they changed its meaning to delegation from below, and thereby contaminated the concept as it was used in the Church and theological reflection.[3]

Instead, we can understand the scope of the terms by stressing the emergence, at the councils of Constance and Basle, of the expression *universalem ecclesiam repraesentans*, applied to the conciliar assembly; the expression was still used in Ferrara in 1438 at the Council moved to that city by order of Eugene IV. The designation of the Council as *repraesentatio ecclesiae* and not just as a solemn form of the exercise of the supreme power of the college of bishops (Code of Canon Law, canon 337, 1), is not a small difference. In the change of terms, what takes place is a shift from mystery to law. The power to represent the whole Church derives from him who 'makes himself present', from Christ the head acting here and now in the Council *directly*. The Council represents the Church because Christ through his Spirit brings about in the Council exactly what he brings about in the whole Church to produce the agreement of hearts in faith and charity.

The shift made by the Code of Canon Law, which reduces the Council to a governance function,[5] reflects the shift of the Church from the dimension of People of God and *communio* to the axis of hierarchy and authority. In contrast, the evolution of the understanding of Christians in the twentieth century has led to a rediscovery of the dimension of the Church as mystery, its dimension as People of God, and of the central place occupied in the Church by the event of *communio*. And it is precisely the renewed consciousness of the Church as sacrament of Trinitarian *communio* that requires an adequate theology and a correct practice of *repraesentatio*. The recovery of the original meaning of the representation of the Church in a council, which means simply the becoming present and active of the reality represented, through the *virtus* proper to it, enables us to understand, not only what is at stake on every occasion, but at the same time the implications of *communio* and the conditions for it to become a reality.

In fact, prior to any other doctrinal or denominational determinations, the history of Christian experience is permeated by the conviction that the glorified Christ makes himself present and operative. Through his Spirit, he continues to 'be in the midst' of those gathered in his name (Matt. 18.20, one of the classic texts of the theology of councils) and makes present the fruits of that Spirit. And just as historically the believing community structures itself internally through ministries, institutions and various activities, the operative presence of Christ comes to be seen not just as a source of legitimation, but also as the foundation of the truth and efficacy of all these structures. Thus in an authentic council the whole Church is made present, not in the sense of human delegation, but because the Spirit himself brings about the consensus and the glorified Christ unites the

Church to himself in what the theology of conciliar liturgy calls a wedding. It was this conviction that was expressed in the words of John XXIII's opening address to the Council, *Gaudet Mater Ecclesia*, when he declared that 'Ecumenical councils, every time they meet, are solemn celebrations of the union of Christ and his Church and so lead to a universal spread of truth, a right ordering of life for individuals, families and society, to a strengthening of spiritual energies, fixing our eyes on the true and eternal blessings.'

It was this aspect of the Council, its representation of the Church as the bride of the glorified Christ, that enabled it to play an active role in the tradition of the Gospel at a decisive moment in human history. This was an epochal moment: the Cold War seemed to have divided the world into two opposed blocs, but the 'signs of the times' mentioned by John XXIII in his encyclical *Pacem in Terris* were beginning to emerge: the socio-economic rise of the working classes, the entry of women into public life, the end of the dichotomy between dominant peoples and dominated peoples, the need for a lasting peace with adequate instruments for promoting and maintaining it. At this epochal moment, the very nature of the Gospel was revealed, its living substance called to nourish every man and every woman, to ask for a new global understanding, a doctrinal penetration for the 'formation of consciences'. Vatican II represented the process of spiritual conversion through which the bishops performed their global reinterpretation of the living substance of the Gospel for their own time, though with the limitations of their grasp of the problems at stake. The Council was thus an act of the tradition that is constantly growing in the Church and in which the Church transmits 'all that she herself is and all that she believes' (*Dei verbum*, 8). In an extremely well chosen phrase, Pope Benedict XVI, in his letter of 10 March 2009 to the bishops on the lifting of the excommunication of the Lefèbvrists, insisted that Vatican II 'bears within itself the whole doctrinal history of the Church'.[6] The immediate context of the letter suggests that this phrase is directed at those who 'present themselves as great defenders of the Council'. I am not one of the 'great', but rather than see the Pope's phrase as a reproof, I read in it the deeper meaning of what the Council was. Vatican II was a privileged moment, in which the *whole* Church was *in actu*, that is, fulfilled its role as an assembly dedicated to the transmission of the Gospel of Jesus of Nazareth received from the apostles. At Vatican II the 'whole' Church performed the *paradosis* or transmission in the same way as the apostles.

III The Church enacted

But what do we really mean when we say that at Vatican II the whole Church, the universal Church, was the tradition of the Gospel in action, and was this because the Spirit brought about agreement among Christians with all their weaknesses, their limited understanding of the issues, in fidelity to the Gospel of Jesus of Nazareth?

First of all, I want to stress the *whole* Church. The stress on 'whole' means various things. These are the most important:

1. At Vatican II, there was a partial contribution from the churches separated from Rome, through their observers. Theirs was not a purely passive presence, but, as they themselves recognized, a presence 'from within'. Cardinal Bea, president of the secretariat for Christian unity, recognized, in his farewell address at the end of the Council, that 'Your stay in Rome has gone far beyond your presence... Many things are well known; many others rightly remain the secrets of those concerned or cloaked in the veil of discretion, essential in this area. But for now it can be said that only gradually, with the passing of time, will we be able to realize fully the great thing that the Lord has done for his Church in this area.'[7]

2. The Second Vatican Council was not just a 'council of bishops' just as perhaps, despite the formulae used, no council has ever been just a council of bishops. That they were the final authority is obvious. But, at the same time, it is incontrovertible that the material contribution and the substance of the debate were also determined by other actors. I simply wish to recall on the one hand the role of public opinion, including Christians, non-Christians and political authorities, who made their voices heard in the Council with regard to the declaration on religious freedom and throughout the debate on the Jews. On the other hand it is impossible to underestimate the role of the theologians. In his *Journal,* Yves Congar noted that he was 'struck' by 'the role played by the theologians. At Vatican I, they played almost no role at all... These theologians exercised a real magisterium.'[7]

3. Finally and most importantly, to say that the whole Church was enacted in Vatican II means that it was a great act of reception of the post-modern theological and ecclesial maturation, a visible reception, even to less acute observers, as a result of the fact that decisive figures of the

theological world, condemned or regarded as suspect before the Council, were among the most influential theological actors in the drafting of the conciliar documents.

The Council was the Church enacted, because the bishops (and theologians) really listened to the Gospel. The best summary of this listening comes in the opening words of the Constitution on Divine Revelation, *Dei verbum*: 'Hearing the Word of God with reverence, and proclaiming it with faith', where we see the indissoluble unity of listening and proclamation, since there can be no real proclamation where there has not first been listening and believing. In this listening, the bishops brought about a true conversion that was transmuted into a capacity for a new understanding of the Gospel itself. This is documented in various bishops' diaries, which are the best evidence of this conversion of hearts and minds.

Another high point in the conciliar event as the *Church enacted* was the listening, not to one or other point of Christian doctrine, but to the tradition of the Gospel in its globality in order to communicate it adequately to the demands of our time. John XXIII is often criticized for a lack of programmatic vision for the Council. It is difficult to establish how much truth there is in this judgment. Even Suenens and Montini, with their insistence on the coordination of the Council's works around the axis Church *ad intra/ad extra* (it was no accident that Montini's main idea was an ecclesiological council), have misled many, since John XXIII's declared intention went in a different direction, of a global representation of the living substance of the Gospel. On this point, it is useless to add comments to his own words, and I shall limit myself to emphasizing what I regard as crucial in these extracts: 'The "salient point" of this Council is thus not a *discussion of one or other article* of the fundamental teaching of the Church, as a general repetition of the teaching of the Fathers or ancient and modern theologians, which we may assume is perfectly present and familiar to our minds. *For this we would not need a Council.* But from the renewed, serene and calm adherence to *all the Church's teaching in its entirety and precision,* as it still shines forth in the council documents of Trent and Vatican I, the Christian, Catholic and apostolic spirit of the whole world, awaits *a leap forward towards a doctrinal penetration and formation of consciences* in more perfect correspondence with faithfulness to authentic doctrine, but including that studied and expounded through the *forms of enquiry and literary formulation of modern thought.* The *substance* of the ancient doctrine of the 'deposit of faith' is one thing, the *formulation in which it is presented* is another, and it is this that must be always borne in mind – with patience if necessary –measuring everything in the forms and propositions of a magisterium that is predominantly pastoral in character.'[8] The history of the Council shows how, in the bishops' interventions, this remained the guiding criterion.

I have examined elsewhere Roncalli's vocabulary, especially its key terms, 'doctrine', 'substance', 'pastoral', *'aggiornamento'*.[9] Here, let it suffice to emphasize once more that for John XXIII the Council's agenda was precisely a doctrinal penetration into the whole Christian tradition to reinterpret it in order to meet the demands of the present. For him, not even the doctrine of the Church was at the top of this agenda and moreover, by himself naming the Council he called Vatican II, wanted to mark the distance between himself and those who thought it should be the continuation of Vatican I.

The Fathers of the Council at first had trouble in getting used to Pope John's language, as can be appreciated from all the discussion on the draft 'on the sources of revelation', which was finally rejected.[10] But, in the end, we can conclude that they rose to the challenge as far as possible with the analysis of the problems available at the time. Eloquent testimonies of this are, in my view (but here opinions differ) *Dei verbum, Sacrosanctum concilium, Unitatis redintegratio, Ad gentes, Nostra aetate* and, in second place, *Dignitatis humanae, Lumen gentium, Gaudium et spes*.

I justify relegating some documents to 'second place' on the following grounds. The recognition of freedom of conscience was too restricted to the sphere of the State and did not include the Church. *Lumen gentium* in Chapter 3 was too influenced by a universalistic ecclesiology and not sufficiently aware of the centrality of local churches, while *Gaudium et spes* lacked an effective historical hermeneutic. More important, *Gaudium et spes* suffers from the lack of an anthropology adequate to the new approach to lived human history, which Congar wanted to be 'pneumatological' and Dossetti 'eschatological'. But in this the Council's weakness reflected the limited theological development of the twentieth century. The theology of the first half of the last century had, we could say, made up the ground that separated it from the anthropology of the modern period, and developed dynamic and open anthropologies in which Christian revelation was not an imposition from outside, but a response to the creature's deepest desire (de Lubac and Rahner and their followers did precisely this in different ways). But theological reflection, having once reached this important milestone in transcending the extrinsicism of neo-scholastic anthropology, stopped there. Lived human history remained beyond the grasp of the various anthropologies of immanence, and by that very fact also beyond their grasp was the biblical anthropology which, to be specific, is that contained in Chapter 8 of Romans, where the cry of the whole creation is bound up with the wait for the freedom of the children of God.

But these comments, written with the benefit of hindsight, are not meant as hostile criticism, or to impugn the real doctrinal penetration achieved by the Fathers of the Council. Vatican II has its inevitable human dimension. It was not perfect. And above all, what I want to insist on is that the Council, like every council in the history of the Church, was the reception of a maturing of Church awareness that had already taken place.

Another decisive aspect of the Council's hermeneutical process was that the *aggiornamento* and the leap forward did not come, at least for the most part, by resorting to modern thought and its categories, but from the *ressourcement* condemned by *Humani generis*, allowing a new access to the ancient sources of the history of Christianity. True, Roncalli himself, in *Gaudet Mater Ecclesia*, had recommended the use of the forms of investigation developed by modern thought and the exponents of *ressourcement* had adopted historical–critical approaches for Scripture and the study of the Fathers. But these approaches allowed people of our time even closer access to the ancient treasure of the Church, and did not cut the umbilical cord through which believers are nourished in the womb of the one and only tradition of the Gospel in the Church.

The aspect of the conciliar hermeneutical event that is still truly innovative was attention to history. In one of his early essays, O'Malley vividly captured the novelty of John XXIII's approach by contrasting it with the opening address of Egidio of Viterbo at Lateran V: 'It is licit for human beings to be changed by sacred things, but not sacred things by human beings.'[11] But even without going so far back in time, there is a clear contrast with Pius XII's *Humani generis*, which held that the attempts of those who wished (*la nouvelle théologie*) to free dogma from the received expressions of Catholic authors of the day and return instead to the Scriptures and the Fathers were not only leading to dogmatic relativism, but already practising it (*reapse*). It confusingly identified the promoters of radical dogmatic progress with theologians who were focused instead on the unbridgeable distance between the mystery and its conceptual expression.

I believe that the most authentic expression of this historical hermeneutic carried out by the Fathers of the Council was *Dei verbum* itself, especially in the introduction and paragraph 2, where it does not separate revelation from the event of hearing it and so introduces history itself as a constitutive element of God's communication of himself to human beings. It nonetheless remains true that the most direct expression of this historical hermeneutic is certainly *Gaudium et spes*, because in the drafting of this Constitution the fundamental attitude was a receptive contemplation of history as the place where God's call to human beings takes place at every moment, with the explicit recognition that 'the Church is not unaware how much it has profited from the history and development of humankind' (*Gaudium et spes*, 44).

Finally, last but not least, the Church was *in actu* because the hermeneutical event of the tradition of the Gospel was a liturgical act. This is true formally: at least when the conciliar assemblies are united around the Gospel in its place of honour, and although the councils, at least the Western councils, have accepted, with some modifications, the Visigothic *ordo*, the council is formally a liturgical act, introduced by that amazing prayer to the Holy Spirit, the *Adsumus*.[12] The prayer introduces us to the twofold dimension of the synodal event: it is a penitential event, in which the Church acknowledges itself to be sinful and in need of forgiveness and conversion, but it is also an event dominated by the gift of the Spirit who makes conversion possible and enlightens hearts. And it should not be forgotten that every 'congregation' at Vatican II began with a celebration of the Eucharist. Of course, it remains to be judged how much of this formally constitutive dimension was existentially assimilated by the Fathers as they carried out their work and how far it influenced their judgments and decisions. But even theology has not sufficiently studied the link between the synodal event and the liturgical dimension,[13] and the liturgical dimension of councils remains a field for further study.

V   Conclusion

It was not my intention to discourse on the doctrine of councils. What I intended was only an interpretation, no doubt partial, of the ecclesiological scope of an event that certainly implies a specific conception of the nature of the Church, but expresses it in *actu exercitu* without venturing into explicit declarations. On a considered view, this has a decisive consequence for the understanding of this Council's reception. I believe that in the first place this does not imply an application of the decrees, although much remains to be done, indeed almost everything as regards Vatican II's most relevant dogmatic contribution, on the sacramental nature of the episcopate and its collegiality.

The Council will have been truly received insofar as the Church enacts itself in the way it chose to do, even through bitter conflicts, at Vatican II. The final characteristic of Vatican II consists in the fact that in it an authentic council was celebrated. The reception of the Council consists also in the Church's being able to be conciliar in all its manifestations. For this to happen there is a need for a further journey of practice and corresponding ecclesiological reflection.

Translated by Francis McDonagh

Notes

1. G. Alberigo, 'Ecclesiologia in divenire. A proposito di Concilio pastorale e di Osservatori acattolici al Vaticano II', in *Transizione epocale. Studi sul Vaticano II*, Bologna, 2009, pp. 325–50.
2. C. Theobald, *La réception du concile Vatican II. I. Accéder à la source*, Paris, 2009.
3. G. Ruggieri, 'Le dynamisme ecclésial de l'eucharistie: repraesentatio, eucharistie, consensus', in J.-M. Van Cangh (ed.), *L'ecclésiologie eucharistique*, Brussels, 2009, pp. 63–4. On the theme of representation, the key study is H. Hofmann, *Repräsentation. Studien zur Wort- und Begriffsgeschichte von der Antike bis in 19. Jahrhundert*, Berlin, 4th ed., 2003.
4. For a different view, cf. *Cristianesimo nella storia*, 32 (2011)/3: 'I sinodi: organi di governo e/o luogo di formazione del consenso nella chiesa?', P. Hünermann & G. Ruggieri (eds).
5. Cf. The text in *Il Regno Documenti*, 54/7 (2009), pp. 193–6
6. Quotation from Alberigo, 'Ecclesiologia in divenire', *op. cit.*, p. 344.
7. Y. Congar, *Mon Journal du concile*, Paris, 2002, I, pp. 136–7.
8. Translated from the Italian text according to the critical edition of A. Melloni, in *Fede Tradizione Profezia. Studi su Giovanni XXIII e sul Vaticano II*, Brescia 1984, pp. 267–8. As is well-known, the Latin text does not correspond exactly to the text written by Pope John himself.
9. G. Ruggieri, 'Appunti per una teologia in papa Roncalli', in *Papa Giovanni*, ed. G. Alberigo, Rome & Bari 1987, pp. 245–71; 'Esiste una teologia di papa Giovanni?', in *Un cristiano sul trono di Pietro. Studi storici su Giovanni XXIII*, Bergamo, 2003, pp. 253–74.
10. G. Ruggieri, 'Il primo conflitto dottrinale', in Giuseppe Alberigo (ed.), *Storia del concilio Vaticano II: II. La fomazione della coscienza conciliare. Il primo periodo e la*

prima intersessione ottobre 1962 – settembre 1963, Italian edition by Alberto Melloni, Bologna, 1996, pp. 259–93.
11. '*Homines immutari per sacra fas est, non sacra per homines.*', J. W. O'Malley, 'Reform, Historical Consciousness and Vatican II's Aggiornamento', *Theological Studies* 32 (1971), 573–601.12. On the *Adsumus* prayer, cf. M. M. Klöckener, 'La prière d'ouverture des conciles Adsumus: de l'Espagne wisigothique à la liturgie romaine d'après Vatican II', in Achille M. Triacca & A. Pistoia (éds), John Paul II, *Mensagem do Santo Padre ao Episcopado do Brasil, Vaticano, 9 de abril de 1986*. São Paulo, 1986, No. 5. Paris, 27–30 Juin 2000, Rome, 2001, pp. 165–98.
13. A first step in this direction is the volume of *Cristianesimo nella storia*, 28/1 (2007), which contains the results of a seminar proposed by G. Alberigo and his posthumous contribution 'Sinodo come liturgia?' (pp. 1–40).

Ressourcement and Reform at Vatican II

JOHN W. O'MALLEY

I Introduction

The Second Vatican Council could not dodge the issue of change. The upsurge in historical scholarship in the nineteenth century had made even modestly educated people aware that customs, political forms, even moral standards, differed in different epochs. Things were not always the way they were in 1962, when the Council opened. The historian's critical eye had turned even to 'sacred subjects', such as Scripture, liturgy, and doctrine, and had shown how the present diverged from the past.

This was a special problem for a Church that professed not to change. How, for instance, was the Church to explain that the doctrine of the Immaculate Conception of the Virgin Mary, defined in 1854, was part of the ancient 'deposit of faith', when it was unknown in the Church until the Middle Ages? Moreover, Pope John XXIII had in effect thrust the problem of change upon the Council, when he asked it to enact emendations to make the Church's message more intelligible and acceptable to modern persons. He asked for change, even though the changes he asked for might be construed as minimal.

It was clear from the beginning, therefore, that the Council could and should make changes as *aggiornamento*. But within what limits and according to what criteria? More broadly and deeply, how does change legitimately take place within the Church? At the Council, such questions were asked and debated, but no responses to them were elaborated in a theologically adequate way. Bishops and theologians spoke of 'development,' using it generically to explain or to palliate the problem. 'Development of doctrine,' a theory that Catholics viewed with deep suspicion, when Newman gave it its classic formulation in 1846, was now broadly accepted but not deeply probed.

In any case, the problem of change simmered beneath the surface throughout the Council, and it underlay many of the Council's most bitter controversies. The well-known tension between 'the majority' and 'the minority' derived to a large extent from it. Virtually every prelate at the Council was ready to agree that some measure of *aggiornamento* was needed and legitimate, but except for change at a superficially minimum level, opinions differed widely. A much more divisive question was whether the Council could change church teaching. For example, could it change the teaching of nineteenth-century popes that 'separation of Church and State' was an evil, even though in certain circumstances it had to be tolerated until a truly Catholic State could be established?

Vatican II was not the first Council to face the problem of change. Because of Protestant accusations that the 'papal Church' had deviated from the teaching of Scripture and devised doctrines not found there, the Council of Trent had to respond. It did so most notably in its teaching on the sacraments, in which it insisted on unbroken continuity with Christ and the apostles. Trent's insistence on no change contributed heavily to the belief among Catholics that the Church did not change, a belief that, as early as the seventeenth century, had become a mantra in apologetics and polemics against the Protestants. No change became a hallmark of modern Catholicism.

Even the Council of Trent, however, had to acknowledge the fact of change in its efforts to reform the Church, or, as the Council most often expressed it, 'to reform the public behavior [*mores*] of the clergy and Christian people'. It did not hesitate to employ repeatedly and without hesitation the traditional term *reformatio* to designate what it was about in this regard. The reform was, however, the reaffirmation of normative enactments from ancient and, presumably, less corrupt times. On a certain level, therefore, even the reform of the Church was a no-change operation. 'The times' changed (for the worse), but the Church did not change.

In the course of the seventeenth century, Protestants bit by bit appropriated reform as particularly their own word and a characteristic of their ethos. Catholics bit by bit acquiesced in that appropriation.[1] Also, bit by bit, the persuasion took hold among Catholics that their Church did not and could not need reform, for, after all, it did not change, certainly not for the worse. That was the situation that prevailed in Catholicism until the mid-twentieth century. When Yves Congar published his *Vraie et fausse réforme dans l'Église* in 1950, the future Pope John XXIII, then nuncio in Paris, allegedly asked: 'Reform of the Church, is that possible?'[2] The result of this situation was that, for all its importance in the history of the Church, there has been remarkably little study of the idea of reform.[3] Shortly after the publication of *Vraie et fausse*, the Holy Office forbade its reprinting and translation into other languages and informed Congar that in the future everything he intended to publish had first to be submitted to the Master General of the Dominican order for censorship. These strictures were just the beginning. In 1954, there was the great clamp-down on the French Dominicans (and Jesuits), which led to Congar being exiled from Paris and forbidden to teach and publish.

Vraie et fausse was not a historical study in the conventional sense, but one of the earliest ventures by a Catholic into historical theology. Such an attempt to correlate doctrine and practice with historical contingencies could not but seem dangerous and cause unease in official circles. Moreover, by that time the very word 'reform' had become anathema for Catholics. In his 'Foreword' Congar noted that 'a veritable curse' seemed to hang over the word.[4] Almost certainly for that reason Congar began to promote the term *ressourcement* instead.

Ressourcement was a neologism coined by the French poet Charles Péguy earlier in the century. It means, as its etymology indicates, a return to the sources, the impulse traditionally associated with the Latin *reformatio*. By the time Congar took up *ressourcement* and gave it currency, it implied, as did *reformatio*, using the past to correct the present. In other words, the return to the sources was not an antiquarian project but was driven, implicitly or explicitly, by an agenda for the present.

Although not given currency until the mid-twentieth century, *ressourcement* perfectly describes the many projects of Catholic scholars in the nineteenth century who explored the history of all 'sacred subjects'. Their projects flourished even in the twentieth century in spite of the draconian measures of the campaign waged by the Holy Office against Modernism, which was identified in part with such historical 'relativism'. The very title of the series of patristic texts published with French translations initiated in 1942 by Henri de Lubac and Jean Daniélou proclaimed their project as *ressourcement*, the *Sources Chrétiennes*. Although that venture is now looked upon with respect, at the time it was viewed with displeasure and suspicion as an unwarranted challenge to Thomism, the supposedly traditional theological mode of the Church.

II Vatican II

Therefore, by the time the Council opened on 11 October 1962, three terms were in circulation among Catholic thinkers to deal with the problem of change: *aggiornamento*, development, and *ressourcement*.[5] Although they somewhat overlapped in meaning, they more directly pointed to three ways change might take place in the Church. In the atmosphere of reluctance to admit change that prevailed strongly at the time of the Council, they operated as soft synonyms for it. Of the three, *aggiornamento* emerged as the term most often invoked to explain the scope of the Council. While undoubtedly of great importance, not simply in terms of certain adjustments to modern conditions but more broadly as a reconciliation with what was valid in modernity, *aggiornamento* was not the mode most profoundly operative in the Council. That role was reserved to development and *ressourcement*.

As the Council was drawing to a close, John Courtney Murray famously commented that 'development of doctrine' was the issue under the issues at Vatican II.[6] In fact, 'development' was a mind-set that pervaded the thinking of the majority at the Council and did so on a much wider scope than doctrine, a fact revealed by how often the Council had recourse to words that expressed it. The Latin equivalents of 'evolution' and 'development' (*evolutio, evolvere*), for instance, occur 42 times in the Council documents. The Latin equivalents of 'progress' and 'advance' (*progredior, progressio, progressus*) occur a whopping 120 times. These are not only among the most characteristic words of Vatican II, but are virtually absent from the vocabulary of previous Councils.

The constitution on divine revelation, *Dei verbum*, was among the most contentious of the Council's enactments, an object of bitter controversy from the moment it was introduced in the first period as *De fontibus revelationis* until the final text was approved just weeks before the Council ended. The minority opposed it on several grounds, among which was an understanding of tradition as an evolving or developing reality, as expressed in No. 8: 'This tradition, which comes from the Apostles, progresses [*proficit*] in the Church under the assistance of the Holy Spirit. There is growth [*crescit*] in understanding of what is handed on, both in the words and the realities they express'. There will come a day when God's truth reaches its fullness [*plenitudinem*] in the Church.[7]

Ressourcement was the third mode of change invoked at the Council.

Although it and development are sometimes operative in the same paragraph or even sentence, they differ in two important respects. First, *ressourcement* implies human agency in the process of change. It is a self-conscious and deliberate undertaking. Development, on the contrary, suggests a process of growth, evolution, or efflorescence in which such agency is absent or at least less self-consciously employed. Development happens, whereas *ressourcement* is an action that makes things happen.

Secondly, they differ in their assessment of the present state of things, in their assessment of the status quo. Development essentially accepts the present as the norm for understanding the past and judging it. It accepts, that is to say, the status quo today as legitimate and normative, and it is thus essentially uncritical regarding it. *Ressourcement*, on the contrary, uses the past to judge and criticize the present and thus to *reform* or change it. None the less, the majority in the Council appealed to both development and *ressourcement* to justify measures that the minority most vigorously and adamantly opposed.

In its employment of *ressourcement,* the majority portrayed itself as the champions of earlier and more genuine traditions and portrayed the minority as trapped in positions of the more recent past. The majority was thus, in its own eyes, more traditional than those who professed to be the traditionalists. The declaration on religious liberty, *Dignitatis humanae*, is an excellent case in point. The majority could not deny that pope after pope, beginning with Gregory XVI in the early nineteenth century, had condemned religious liberty, freedom of conscience, and separation of Church and State.

The prelates and theologians of the majority justified their position on two grounds. First, in the West the rabidly anti-clerical secular State, which was the enemy against which the popes elaborated their position, was now a thing of the past, as was clear from the dominant role 'Christian democracy' was playing in the politics of many countries since the end of World War II. The times had changed, and therefore this *aggiornamento* was legitimate.

Secondly, the most traditional and fundamental teaching of the Church, as justified from Scripture and the earliest Christian sources, was that the act of faith had to be free and that conscience was, for the individual, the inner law that, even if erroneous, had to be obeyed. In its very first paragraph, the declaration almost explicitly invoked *ressourcement*: the Council 'examines the sacred tradition and teaching of the Church, from which it continually draws new insights in harmony with the old.'[8] The hard core of the minority never bought this explanation, and even today the Society of St Pius X rejects *Dignitatis humanae*, because it contradicts nineteenth-century papal teaching. Such teaching, according to them, cannot be changed.

By far the most contentious issue at the Council was the doctrine of episcopal collegiality. The minority saw it as utterly incompatible with papal infallibility as defined in Vatican I, and as a pernicious diminishment of the Petrine office. For them it was, moreover, a thinly veiled revival of conciliarism, a doctrine the popes had repeatedly and roundly condemned. These were powerful arguments.

In the decades before the Council, scholars had shown that in the Middle Ages there were several realities later gathered under the category of conciliarism, that at least one of these was accepted by canonists and theologians as perfectly orthodox, and that it was only through some form of conciliarism that Church was rescued from the Great Western Schism (1378–1417).

The majority, with greater or lesser clarity, then appealed to the ancient synodal tradition of the Church, and, more pointedly, to the authority Jesus conferred not only on Peter but on the Twelve. Collegiality was reconcilable, therefore, with the primacy. These arguments were clearly *ressourcement* in that they were derived from authoritative 'sources'. As *ressourcement*, they also evinced the impulse central to *reformatio* of a correction of the status quo or a moderation of it by way of improvement. In other words, they were marshalled to effect a 'change for the better', *mutatio in melius*, the classic definition of *reformatio*.

Although *ressourcement* and *reformatio* might be taken in many cases as almost synonymous, the Council itself was inclined to tread warily. In its sixteen final documents it applied *reformatio* to the Church only once, in the often quoted line from the decree on ecumenism, *Unitatis redintegratio* (No. 6): 'In its pilgrimage on earth Christ summons the Church to continual reformation [*reformationem*], of which it is always in need, in so far as it is an institution of human beings here on earth.'[9] That was a bold statement in the early 1960s and was recognized as such at the time.

Instead of 'reform' the Council preferred euphemisms such as 'renewal' or 'renovation' (*renovatio*) a term that occurs 64 times, most often to indicate changes in church life or practice, that is, to indicate some aspect of reform of the Church. This queasiness about *reformatio* explains why, even almost a half-century after the close of the Council, Catholics continued to show a decided preference for softer words when referring to Vatican II. It was a Council of 'updating' or even 'modernizing.' It was a Council of 'renewal.' It was anything but a *reform* Council!

On 22 December 2005, that situation changed dramatically. In his now famous address to the Roman Curia on that day Pope Benedict XVI proposed that the proper lens for understanding Vatican II was a 'hermeneutic of reform'.[10] In that instant reform was immediately and powerfully rehabilitated. It was authoritatively readmitted into Catholic theological vocabulary. The way was now opened for historical and theological examination of it as applied to Vatican II.

In his address, the Pope did not rest content with merely introducing the term. He went on at some length to explain what he understood it to entail. In so doing he implicitly reinforced the point made by Congar in 1950 that the term is 'a little vague' (*un peu vague*) and by Gerhart Ladner a few years later that it is multivalent.[11] What reform means in concrete circumstances, that is to say, is not self-evident. It is revealed only when tested against the historical phenomena it professes to describe.

Scholars immediately set themselves to analyse the papal address and especially to try to divine just how this new hermeneutic related to the 'hermeneutic of continuity' that it replaced in the paradigm Pope Benedict as Cardinal Ratzinger had insisted upon for the previous 20 years, beginning with the famous *Ratzinger Report* published in 1985.[12] Not surprisingly, strong affinities emerged between the new term and the old.

Present in the address, for instance, was the rejection of a 'hermeneutic of rupture' as an instrument of interpretation for Vatican II. 'The Church is, as much before as after the Council, the same Church.'[13] On this point, the Pope would find little disagreement except from members of the Society of St Pius X, who deem the Council heretical. Yet, such statements weight the address heavily towards a no significant change interpretation. The pontiff's distinction between 'principles' that do not change and are not subject to contingencies, and contingencies themselves, which of course by definition do change, weight it the same way. We should not be deceived, Pope Benedict warns, by 'apparent discontinuities'.

The address blurs, moreover, the distinction between the three categories of *aggiornamento*, development, and reform. In fact, at points it seems to identify reform with development [*sviluppo*], which ratifies the status quo. The pontiff can hardly be faulted for such blurring because it is still common among interpreters of the Council, and in fact it does not lack a certain basis in historical reality itself. In concrete instances these three modes often overlap and are operative at the same time. Nonetheless, the distinction among them is crucial for a fruitful exploration of the implications of a 'hermeneutic of reform'.

The confluence of the three categories and the importance the pontiff implicitly attaches to it has an important consequence: validation of the *dynamic* character of the Council's enactments, a dynamism many conservative commentators have denied and decried. This dynamism thus also becomes a legitimate subject for exploration. It promises to be as revealing about the character of the Council as the related question of the distinction between the three categories.

In any case, we need to remember that the address on 22 December 2005, was, after all, an address, not a theological treatise. We should not expect it to provide a full and fully elaborated 'theology of the hermeneutics of reform'. Such an elaboration is, rather, the task the address has opened up for theologians and historians.

In that regard, what is perhaps most helpful in the address is the definition Pope Benedict offers of reform: 'The nature of true reform consists precisely in this blending, at different levels, of continuity and discontinuity.[14] That is a fine working definition, a definition in accord with *ressourcement* as its proponents at the Council understood it. With it, theologians and historians now have licence to address the Council with a category that was off limits formerly. In so doing, they can assess in each instance the degree of continuity and discontinuity respectively present, and thereby judge just how wide and deep (or how narrow and superficial) the reform of Vatican II was. Reform is, as mentioned, multivalent and 'a little vague'. It does not have content except through the contingencies which it tries to explain in each instance.

Notes

1. See J. W. O'Malley, *Trent and All That: Renaming Catholicism in the Early Modern Era*, Cambridge, MA, 2000, pp. 16–45.
2. P. Philibert, 'Translator's Introduction', in Yves Congar, *True and False Reform in the Church*, Collegeville, MN, 2011, p. xi.
3. There have been, of course, many exceptions, beginning with Gerhart Ladner, *The Idea of Reform: Its Impact on Christian Thought and Action in the Age of the Fathers*,

Cambridge, MA, 1959. See also, for example, Konrad Repgen, '"Reform" als Leitgedanke kirchlicher Vergangenheit und Gegenwart', *Römische Quartalschrift für christliche Altertumskunde und Kirchengeschichte*, 84 (1989), pp. 5–39; J. W. O'Malley, 'Developments, Reforms, and Two Great Reformations: Towards a Historical Assessment of Vatican II', *Theological Studies* 44 (1983), pp. 373–406.
4. Y. Congar, *Vraie et fausse réforme dans l'Église*, Paris, 1950, p. 13, '*une véritable malédiction.*'
5. See J. W. O'Malley, *What Happened at Vatican II*, Cambridge, MA, pp. 36–41, 299–303.
6. J. C. Murray, 'This Matter of Religious Freedom', *America*, 9 January 1965, p. 43.
7. N. Tanner (ed.), *Decrees of the Ecumenical Councils*, vols I & II,' Washington, DC, 1990, 2:974.
8. *Ibid.*, 2:1002.
9. *Ibid.*, 2:913.
10. *Acta Apostolicae Sedis: Commentarium Officiale,* 98 (2006), pp. 40–53, at 45–53. Henceforth, 'Papal Address'.
11 Ladner, *Idea of Reform*, pp. 9–31.
12. See, e.g., Joseph A. Komonchak, 'Benedict XVI and the Interpretation of Vatican II,' *Cristianesimo nella Storia*, 28 (2007), pp. 323–37; Lieven Boeve, 'La vraie réception de Vatican II n'a pas encore commencé', Joseph Ratzinger, 'Révélation et autorité de Vatican II', in Gilles Routhier & Guy Jobin, (eds), *L'autorité et les autorités: L'herméneutique théologique de Vatican II*, Paris, 2010, pp. 13–50; Karim Schelkens, 'La réception de "Dei Verbum" entre théologie et histoire,' *ibid.*, pp. 51–68.
13. Papal Address, p. 51: 'La Chiesa è, tanto prima quanto dopo il Concilio, la stessa Chiesa, una, santa, . . .' My translation, as also below.
14. *Ibid.*, p. 49: 'È proprio in questo insieme di continuità e discontinuità a livelli diversi che consiste la natura della vera riforma'.

Vatican II Confronts the Unknown Collegial Discernment of the 'Signs of the Times'

CHRISTOPH THEOBALD SJ

Fifty years after the opening of the Second Vatican Council, it is not easy to recall the uncertainty that reigned during those summer and autumn months of 1962, when a future new beginning for the Church was being decided. Nothing had been put into writing yet, but the mass of texts produced by preparatory commissions almost exclusively dominated by neo-Thomist thinking suddenly filled the 'space' deliberately provided by John XXIII, when he gave the future Council a relatively open objective (Christian unity and the reform of Catholicism). On the very evening of 11 October, Yves Congar noted in his journal: 'To all intents and purposes, scholasticism has penetrated the government of the Roman Curia. The preparatory commissions reflect this state of affairs…But scholasticism has scarcely affected the pastoral government of the dioceses, and that is to the fore now'.[1]

Recalling this disturbing and delicate situation at the beginning of the Council helps us today to guard against the risk of reducing it to a finished collection of documents. The absence of official texts throughout the whole of the first period (except for John XXIII's addresses and the conciliar Fathers' message to all humanity) helps us to appreciate a new way of proceeding (the 'pastoral government' of the Church to which Congar refers) that only gradually took shape after bitter conflicts. This collegial way of discerning the signs of the times, under the unique authority of the Word of God, would only be codified two, even three, years later. Acquired customs and the unknown future produced a wide range of anxieties and power games. It was some time before they could adjust to one another and eventually become real listening to the Word of God and what people in the contemporary world, observers and others, had to say to the Church. This is the simultaneously individual and collective process of learning and conversion which the Council transmitted to us before issuing any texts. It is the conciliar process which is so immensely appropriate to the sometimes worrying unknown future that faces us today.

I 'To interpret the signs of the times…'

We should begin with Jesus' advice (Matt. 16.1–4), which John XXIII repeated in his message to the Council. It is a guideline running through all the Council's work, from the apostolic constitution *Humanae salutis* of 25 December 1961 convoking the Council to the pastoral constitution promulgated on 7 December 1965.

The first official mention of the task of recognizing the signs of the times is found in the convocation. There it is already linked to Jesus' commandment in Matthew to go and make disciples of all nations (Matt. 28.19), an injunction immediately retranslated in contemporary terms: 'The beneficial influence of the Council deliberations must, as we sincerely hope, succeed to the extent of imbuing with Christian light and penetrating with fervent spiritual energy not only the intimacy of the soul but the whole collection of human activities'.[2] This call is borne, according to John XXIII, by the 'consoling presence' of Christ (Matt. 28.20): 'And remember, I am with you always, to the end of the age', 'above all in the most grave periods of humanity'. It is in such circumstances that we have to heed his exhortation to interpret the 'signs of the times', which the pope does with a 'vigilance' completely opposed to the 'discouragement' of those 'who only see darkness totally enveloping our world'. He does not succumb to blind optimism, when he 'distinguishes in the midst of so much darkness numerous signs which augur well for the fate of the Church and of humanity'. His perception of reality is governed by his 'confidence' in the presence of Christ that enables him to see that 'humanity is at the turning point of a new era'; that from now on the proclamation of the Gospel can rely on the questions and aspirations, and even a greater maturity, of humanity; and that the Church has already begun to transform and renew itself when confronted with the development of human societies.

These simultaneously biblical, spiritual and theological guidelines seem very odd, when compared with the neo-scholastic attitude of the vast majority of 60 preparatory schemas, some of which had begun to circulate among the future Fathers of the Council from the summer of 1962, to their considerable distress. This was probably why some theologians, such as Chenu and Congar, took the initiative in September and wrote a 'message to all humanity', which Chenu described in a letter to Karl Rahner as a 'declaration...in the style of the Gospel, in the prophetic perspectives of the Old and New Testaments, and addressed to a humanity where greatness and distress, in spite of failures and errors, represent an aspiration to the light of the Gospel'.[3] Reworked by four French bishops (or 'drowned in holy water', as Chenu would have it), this text was put before the Council on 20 October and offered the opportunity for a first controversial debate, before being promulgated.

As yet it does not mention collegiality but emphasizes the conciliar subject in a biblical and patristic perspective while bringing out the purpose of the Council by reference to the Pope's opening address. The task of discerning the 'signs of the times' is not named as such, but the message firmly evokes the fact that the bishops have assembled in Rome *together with* those who have been entrusted to their care: 'Coming together in unity from every nation under the sun, we carry in our hearts the hardships, the bodily and mental distress, the sorrows, longings and hopes of all the peoples entrusted to us. We urgently turn our thoughts to all the anxieties by which modern humanity is afflicted'. The ultimate aim is to respond today to 'the divine plan, that through love God's kingdom may already shine out on earth in some fashion as a preview of God's eternal kingdom'.[4]

It was necessary to wait for the final revisions of 'The Church in the Modern World' (*Gaudium et spes*), before this perspective became a 'method' or 'mode of procedure', the one, in fact, which the Council adopted throughout its labours, and which it has handed on to those who take their inspiration from it today:[5] 'The People of God believes that it is led by the Spirit of the Lord who fills the earth. Motivated by this faith, it labours to decipher authentic signs of God's presence and purpose in the happenings, needs and desires in which this People has a part along with other men of our age. For faith throws a new light on everything, manifests God's design for man's total vocation, and thus directs the mind to solutions which are fully human.' (GS 11, par. 1).

I shall briefly recall some elements of this discernment. First, it relies on a basic principle in the proclamation of the Gospel already at work in those who will receive it; an evangelical reality is not only at work in individuals but in the culture of those who are to be its recipients. The reception of this

Good News is not an act of servile submission to a purely external message but has to do with a freedom liberated from its own innermost depths by what is heard. What happened between Jesus and the men and women who, having crossed his path, also went on to say: 'My son, my daughter, it is *your* faith that has saved you', still applies today when Christians meet other people and perceive and discern what is at work in them, for the archetypal 'messianic sign' is 'faith', the very sign 'of the presence and design of God'.

But this 'faith' is also *a 'faith' which interprets* reality. It must be so, because reality is essentially obscure and we can only gain access to it at the cost of a necessarily arduous process of decipherment. Far from imposing their own interpretation of reality on others, the conciliar Fathers tried to engage in a collective process of re-reading which obeyed strict rules; the preliminary account of *Gaudium et spes* on 'The Situation of People in the Modern World' (GS 4–10) is a practical expression of it. But they also engaged in it with their own resources: their tradition, the Scriptures in pride of place, and above all their sense of 'faith'. They perceived it and discerned it in others, while allowing those others to find their own words to express it, sometimes offering them words drawn from their own history.

This process of interpretation is guided by a threefold process, marked out by the three key words of *Gaudium et spes* (11): events, needs, and desires. 'Faith' takes shape in confrontation with unforeseen 'events'; Luke's Gospel already underlined this, when he evoked in his dedication 'the events that have been fulfilled among us' (Luke 1.1), and history has given practical expression to this purely descriptive aspect of faith, today as yesterday. Then, whether individual or collective, these events make known 'needs' which are sometimes as colossal as the current ecological challenge. These are needs or necessities which demand considerable 'faith' energy to confront them and simultaneously release that energy. There are salient 'wishes' or 'desires' that manifest themselves in connection with this or that event, and which arouse the 'messianic' orientation of humanity implied in 'God's design', often in unexpected and sometimes distorted ways. *Gaudium et spes* (11) depends on the desire for 'fully human solutions'. In the modern era and at the Council (for example in the debate with and about Marxism) this utopian vision has led to terrible conflicts and will always provoke them; but the sign of 'faith' is still discernible there. This faith cannot persist without perception and opens up, in our often blocked situations, breaches where, however small they might be, another and better future is proclaimed.

II   ...subject to the authority of the Word of God...

In the autumn of 1962, this mode of procedure was not yet codified, although it had already been at work within the assembly since the debate about the conciliar message. There was still a major obstacle to deal with: the culture, and even a certain Catholic cultural way of thinking, that risked preventing people from hearing out not only the 'joys and sadness, hopes and anguish of people of our own times', but (also and simultaneously) the Word of God. This was the main question of the first period that aroused the consciences of the Fathers of the Council: first of all on the debate on the renewal of the liturgy, and especially, the liturgical use of the vernacular, and then, at a more basic level, in the difficult discussion on the 'sources of Revelation' and the place of tradition in listening to the God who 'converses' today with the Church and with all humanity.

This was the start of a difficult collective learning process in listening: not only a 'dual' listening process (listening to the Word of God *and* listening to 'what is genuinely human' in society [GS 1]), but listening to some very complex and discordant 'voices' of 'tradition' in the ecumenical sense: the 'voices' of our predecessors that risk being heard so loudly that we no longer hear the Word of God addressed to modern people. Two witnesses with very different viewpoints help us to understand the spiritual point at issue in this major conflict at the Council. At the end of the first period of the Council, Cardinal Lercaro introduced the Lucan principle of 'evangelization of the poor.' In 1964, he very freely developed the cultural and historical aspects of this principle: 'Today the moment has come for a clearer *de facto* separation of the Church and its fundamental message from a certain "cultural system and approach" whose eternal applicability and universality have been firmly defended by many ecclesiastics, prompted by a feeling of self-important proprietorship'.[6] On the other hand, one of the principal defenders of the preparatory schemas, Monsignor Joseph Clifford Fenton, a peritus at the Council, reports in his diary that, after the famous withdrawal of the 'two-source' schema, the men from Cardinal Ottaviani's team were convinced that they were living in 'daemonic times'.[7]

It was not until 1965 that the Council managed to establish a 'rule' that would not exempt any of the recipients from the complex, never perfect experience of individual and collective listening to *three* simultaneous 'voices'.[8] In its presentation of the process of 'tradition', *Dei verbum*, the constitution on divine revelation, also emphasized the process of 'reception': the apostles 'handed on what they had received (*acceperant*) from the lips of Christ, from living with him, and from what he did or what they had learned (*didicerant*) through the prompting of the Holy Spirit' (DV 7). This 'apprenticeship' would remain appropriate thereafter (*Ecclesia didicit*), because, as *Gaudium et spes*, the pastoral constitution on the Church in the world, decrees: 'Indeed this accommodated preaching of the revealed Word ought to remain the law (*lex*) of all evangelization' (GS 44, par. 2). The decree on the missionary activity of the Church, promulgated the same day, would even go so far as to stipulate that, in a new cultural situation, 'a fresh scrutiny will be bought to bear on the deeds and words which God has made known,' (*Ad gentes* 22). In fact, by 'revealing and communicating himself' (DV 2 & 6), God delivers himself entirely as a mystery into human hands. This truly spectacular and cataclysmic event is a 'theologal' counterweight to the seismic transformation brought about by the innovatory aspects of the modern world and the growing awareness of people everywhere that they are heirs to a tiny planet of no importance in an all but infinite universe.

III   ...the collegial way

Clearly, the only way to confront this transformation through faith is communality and, with regard to apostolic authority, collegiality. This was made clear even before the Council confronted the difficult question of the status to be given to this episcopal collegiality, and of the role and freedom to be assigned to the Petrine ministry at the heart of this college. In fact, before this question was posed explicitly, the everyday administration of the Council had already addressed it and disseminated a more or less credible image of it to the outside world.

John XXIII set himself a rule to follow that was in perfect accordance with the pastoral principle. He told Cardinal Suenens that 'The main duty of the pope is to listen and to be silent in order to give the Holy Spirit free reign'.[9] An entry for 19 November 1962 in his journal *Pater Amabilis* reads: 'Today once again, interesting to hear all the interventions. For the main part they are critical of the proposed schemas (Cardinal Ottaviani), which were prepared together by many hands, but reveal the somewhat predominant obsession of one person and an unswerving mentality that just cannot relinquish the style of scholastic instruction. The partial blindness of one eye casts a shadow on the overall vision. Of course, the reaction is strong, sometimes too strong. *But I think that harmony will eventually prevail*'.[10]

But what was to be done when some of those present – a far from insignificant minority – refused to proceed like that and even called the rules of procedure into question, citing a previous 'dogmatic' agreement, and provoked a series of strategies and counter-strategies? This limit point was reached on several occasions, in particular on 25 February 1963, when Cardinal Ottaviani opposed the vote of the mixed Commission on *De revelatione*, and questioned Cardinal Bea's loyal attachment to the Catholic faith; and again in November 1964, when the minority represented the orientation vote of 30 October on the sacramental nature of episcopacy and on collegiality as irregular, and accused the majority of trying to turn the opinion of one school of theology into dogma (which was an argument that the majority had already used to contest the minority's dogmatization of the two-source theory of Scripture and revelation).

In fact, the result was a 'paradigmatic conflict' about the interpretation of the entire Catholic faith. The conciliar assembly and the two conciliar popes, John XXIII and Paul VI, gradually discovered that the adoption of an evangelical or collegial mode of procedure, though in accordance with the truth pursued by everyone there in concert, cold never be imposed anywhere by any procedural rules, but must result from a non-programmable conversion of all participants. The only 'limit' necessary with regard to the theologal freedom of this conversion was the necessary efficiency of an assembly of inordinately vast proportions and the time which it had available. Therefore a 'compromise' would be called for in a certain number of cases, without damaging the prophetic character of the Council in any way. The pentecostal way of ensuring that people were 'heard' within historical limits would appeal to the eventual audience.

It not until autumn 1964 that this collegial way of proceeding was codified, as it was in the decree on ecumenism (11) accompanying the Constitution on the Church, which gave it something like a 'rule of interpretation' requiring accordance between the truth and the way in which people sought it *together*: 'Thus the way will be opened whereby this kind of fraternal rivalry will incite all to a deeper realization and a clearer expression of the unfathomable riches of Christ (cf. Eph. 3.8)'.

* * *

When he re-read an account of the first period of the Council on 6 December 1962, Cardinal Lercaro noted that 'two months of work and *really humble, free and fraternal research* have brought us to the point where we understand better and *all together* what the second Vatican Council should suggest to the people of this era'.[11] Fifty years on, the issue of 'agreeing' about the finality of the Council remains the same, but in a profoundly different world. The 'pastoral government' of the Church should try to bring about a collegial way of discerning the signs of the times, under the sole authority of the Word of God. This proposition calls for an apprenticeship and conversion that cannot be demanded but depend on grace, the 'abundant grace' of God.

Translated by J. G. Cumming

Notes

1. Yves Congar, *Mon journal du Concile I,* Paris, 2002, p. 109.
2. Jean XXIII et Paul VI, *Discours au Concile,* Paris, 1966, p. 27.
3. M.-D. Chenu, *Notes quotidiennes au Concile. Journal de Vatican II, 1962–1963*, Paris, 1995, p. 57.
4. *AS* I/1, 254.
5. For a more detailed account, see C. Theobald, 'La réception du concile Vatican II, vol. I. Accéder à la source', in *Unam sanctam*, new series 1, Paris, 2009, pp. 778–93; 819–34.
6. S III.6, 251.
7. Monsignor Fenton's diary, quoted by G. Ruggieri, in G. Alberigo (ed.), *Histoire du concile Vatican II. 1959–1965.* II, *La formation de la conscience conciliaire,* Paris, 1998, p. 409.
8. For a more detailed account, see 'La réception du concile Vatican II', vol. I, *op. cit.*, pp. 290–319, 719.
9. Angelo Giuseppe Roncalli–John XXIII, *Pater amabilis. Agende del pontefice. 1958–1963,* Bologna, 2007, p. 457.
10. *AS* I.4, 327 (my emphasis).
11. *AS* I.4, 327 (my emphasis).

Vatican II between Catholicism and Catholicity

GÉRARD SIEGWALT

I Vatican II: between Catholicism and catholicity

Catholicity has always been, and remains, the challenge which Vatican II poses for Roman Catholicism. The challenge of catholicity also concerns Protestant churches of all persuasions and the Orthodox communion.

Although I am a Protestant theologian, this article is more than a comment from outside Catholicism. '*Nostra res agitur*', said Willem Visser't Hooft, the Secretary General of the World Council of Churches, when John XXIII announced the Second Vatican Council – 'It concerns us too', which means the Protestant churches, including the Anglican communion, and the Orthodox churches. This article is essentially restricted to Roman Catholicism, and to the challenge which Vatican II represents for it, but to some extent, it also concerns the main families of Protestant churches and Orthodoxy. Indeed, in the other Christian churches, especially in the various Protestant churches, there are all kinds of connections with what I have to say here about Roman Catholicism and catholicity. But these points will be not so much explicit as implicit, since they are not the direct object of these remarks of a Protestant theologian on Vatican II.

The significance and legitimacy of this approach are related to the unity of Christ's Church. The source of these comments and thus their criterion, is the Church of Christ and more precisely Christ himself. They all refer to him and to one another, because each of them in its specificity, and in spite of all due ambiguity, possesses something of the Church of Christ. Mutually critical dialogue nourished by the relation to Christ is part of their very nature. It is a requirement of truth, because it is fraternal, and a requirement of fraternity, because it is true. Any spirit of superiority and thus of arrogance in any Christian body with regard to any other is as uncharacteristic as mutual indifference. John XXIII invited observers from non-Roman churches to the Council. Dialogue presupposes and implies a reciprocal participation which, when successful, is a mark of the Church of Christ at the heart of human society taking effect in and between churches. The following has two main aspects: the innovatory nature of Vatican II and the challenge which it poses.[1]

II The innovatory nature of Vatican II

An event like Vatican II calls for several approaches which are usually variants of two different though not mutually exclusive viewpoints, one historical and the other theological. Each of them tends to take priority at the expense of the other, or the two together try to dominate a field whose actual nature they ignore. This tendency to absolutization is a flight into history or into theology, or even into both simultaneously. It is an escape from reality. Both forms of flight were characteristic of whole areas of traditional Roman Catholicism before Vatican II. Admittedly traditional Roman Catholicism cannot be entirely reduced to these aspects; nevertheless, but its authentic spiritual reality can only benefit from an analysis of this kind.

Flight into history: that is: the history of the foundations of Christian faith and of the Christian Church, and of the Judaeo-Christian sacred Scriptures, and the history of the Councils and of characteristic aspects of the Church, but also the isolation and thus absolutization of this history in relation to general history.

Flight into theology: that is: the theological absolutization of history understood as above, and of Holy Scriptures, Councils, and characteristic aspects of the Church. Since history is conceived of essentially as referring to the past, this inclination tends towards fundamentalism (absolutization of the foundations of the Christian faith and Church, and of the Scriptures), and/or towards integrism (absolutization of this aspect of the history of the Church); in other words, towards restoration of the past, with 'salvation lies in the past' as the watchword. The past is considered to be supportive and a vital impetus in the present, and there is a tendency to adapt the past to the present, to develop the potential of the past, and to 'actualize' it: salvation is to be sought in the present efficacy of the past. A tendency to flight is also apparent in mystical theology, when it is diluted in a form of disembodied spiritualism, or is conceived of as a refuge from reality considered as the locus of evil.

III The threefold temptation of traditional Catholicism

Over the centuries, traditional Roman Catholicism has been subject to a threefold temptation:

1. the absolutized particularism of the idea it has of itself, considered as self-sufficient, either intensively or *ad intra* (in a communitarian sense), in either the extensive or the *ad extra* sense with a pretention to universalism, or both: it is theocratic in both forms;

2. the supranaturalism of its notion of God, who rules the world (and the Church) from without; here we might talk of the extrinsic nature of divine revelation and therefore of the exteriority of the transcendent compared with the immanent; then salvation (which was given in the past and is actualized in the present) originates in another world, a supranatural world (*supra naturam*);

3. the a-historicism of mystical theology as a theology of the experience of God, although that is considered to be located apart from and outside the world.

With reference to the temptations of Roman Catholicism, a temptation in the present context is a tendency to decline, and to go astray from reality. The threefold temptation of traditional Roman Catholicism, and therefore of a period before Vatican II, is certainly still a temptation for conciliar Catholicism, marked by Vatican II yet subsequent to it. Vatican II can be assessed either in terms of these temptations (and then it, or rather its innovatory aspect, is seen as a parenthesis in the history of Roman Catholicism, which is inevitably called on to repair the hiatus); or, on the contrary, in terms of its innovatory character (and therefore of the way in which it tends to move beyond the threefold temptation of the Roman Catholicism that preceded it). Vatican II makes Roman Catholicism confront the question of its possible renewal: the question is that of its catholicity. Vatican II is an issue for Catholicism, because catholicity is an issue for it.

IV An act of conversion to the God of reality

The question, or issue, has to do with the innovatory nature of Vatican II, which consists in the Council's critically positive acceptance of the challenge of reality. Vatican II defined a new approach for history and theology, which could not be reduced to the dominant attitudes of traditional Catholicism. Vatican II emphasized not only the specific history of the faith tradition behind Catholicism but history in general, and simultaneously included (this, at least, was the intention) the other churches, other religions and all humankind in its field of vision. It no longer focused on a supranatural God proper to a 'religion of authority', but a God who is concerned with and linked to this world and humanity, and whose transcendence is thereby shown to be inherent in the immanent as a transcendence of immanence. It is neither merely a form of faith refuge, as in the fundamentalist and integrist tendency bent on restoration, nor simply a faith that actualizes and adapts the fundamental elements of the past, but a faith-source. It does indeed imply the fundamental data handed down from the past but also moves beyond them, since God is the living God. He is, as the Book of Revelation puts it, the one 'who is [that is, today, and on that basis we approach, recognize and bear witness to him as the one] who was and who is coming' (Rev. 1.4). The source is a source of inspiration and orientation, and the living basis for the renewal of life, for it offers us the possibility of living in a new way in and through the given conditions of life, and therefore of reality.

The new approach of Vatican II has to do with the essential correlation between the Church and churches, Christianity and other religions; between the particular and the universal; between God and the world; between transcendence and immanence; and between faith and reality. In this approach, there is no flight into an exclusivist particularism, a doctrinaire and dogmatic theology, or an isle of reclusion for the blessed, all three being versions of a fundamental dualism. Vatican II marked the Roman Church's recognition of reality and of the challenge which it represented for the Church, its self-understanding, and its understanding of God and of faith. At Vatican II, the Catholicism of the second half of the twentieth century reached humanity as it had come to be, aware of the end of its multisecular pretence of constructing another world alongside the real world or in order to master the real world. Vatican II was an act of humanity on the part of the Roman Catholic Church, a new understanding of the real world as a reality inhabited, in spite of all its ambiguity, by God, and an act of conversion to the God of reality.

V The challenge of Vatican II

The innovatory aspect of Vatican II was also its challenge, which was to reconcile Roman Catholicism with catholicity, and catholicity with Roman Catholicism. Vatican II wished to be a Council not of excommunication but of union and communion; not of delimitation but of integration.

Traditional Roman Catholicism, characterized as absolutized particularism, is a Church of delimitation and therefore of exclusion. The delimitation in question is directed outwards, to external reality: this is an inimical confrontation between two regimes, the spiritual and the temporal, although the latter claims to be independent of the former. The history of this confrontation is a long one. It ranges from the medieval investitures dispute to what has been called the Modernist crisis, which, generally speaking, is the conflict between the Roman Catholic Church and the modern world. When confronted by the real external world (external because it refuses to be integrated by the Church), the Church delimited itself as a church in relation to what it is not. This delimitation also took place with regard to what lay and took place within the Church itself. This Church was actually dispersed between East and West and their respective attitudes, one characterized by a predominantly Platonist and thus contemplative Greek philosophy, the other by the Roman and therefore legalistic spirit of organization, yet it had resolutely maintained a fundamental unity throughout the centuries, that is, in its faith, though this was formal, apparent and already suffering from the strain of divisive unrest associated with differences of culture and thus of nations and history, which were distinctive features. Eventually this conflict of specific traits led to a great rupture in the Great Schism of 1054 between East and West. It was followed in the sixteenth century, at the time of the Protestant Reformation, with a schism within Western Christianity. A series of other (quantitatively less emphatic) schisms between the two dominant aspects produced (at the cost of excommunications), or suffered, by the Roman Catholic Church would continue to mark the period beyond the sixteenth century, although the Protestant churches could scarcely be said to have been outclassed in this respect. The adage '*extra ecclesiam nulla salus*' (no salvation outside the Church), though actually inimical to the pretentions of the Roman Catholic Church to spiritual hegemony over the temporal, was directed against the temporal and against the churches cut off from Rome. In fact, the theology of delimitation, with its associated exclusivism, is an ideology justifying the Roman Catholic Church's inability to be the Church in itself alone and, as such, the equal counterpart of the surrounding society and culture. The pretended power and authority advanced by that theology, and the resulting negation of catholicity, serve to compensate for this impotence.

Vatican II started from that point, from the break between the Roman Catholic Church and wider human society, and from the division between the churches, in awareness of the collapse of the walls that had been under way for so long already. Vatican II was produced by the shaking walls of Roman Catholic particularism. The Council was faced by the challenge of having to scrutinize traditional Roman Catholicism to discover the elements that still maintained, and perhaps always would maintain, Christ's authentic Church, God's true revelation and true faith, and of having to separate them from the rest at the great risk of throwing the baby out with the bath water, which might prove to be a remedy worse than the evil to be cured. The challenge of Vatican II was to discern the very heart of authentic Christianity in Roman Catholicism, which had to be cleansed of all kinds of waste matter while confirming its truth and therefore its catholicity, without which it could not be reconciled with the surrounding society and culture or with the other churches.

VI   The beginning of an era of perception of reality

How are we to overcome the exclusivist theology of the delimitation, and therefore of the construction and maintenance of dividing walls, without denying the principle of exclusion inherent in the Christian Church, the revelation of God, and faith? In fact Christianity introduces a difference, which it must respect or deny itself: it is not a form of inclusivism, which is conformism. But that does not make it exclusivist, for the principle of exclusion inherent in Christianity is dialectically linked to the principle of inclusion: exclusion serves inclusion. It is not absolute in the sense of the absolutism characteristic of exclusivism, which fixes the differences, exacerbates them and sets the salient parts against each other, but it relates to the inclusion of what is different inasmuch as it forms part of reality. The relativity of the principle of exclusion is not relativism; the principle of exclusion is a critical principle and therefore a principle of discernment with regard to reality.

A flight from reality, then, is characteristic of a number of the dominant aspects of traditional Roman Catholicism. This flight is a repression, and the repressed content, at the cost of a dualism reinforced by an ideology, is held in a world apart. This is discredited on the basis of ideological prejudice. Reality is subject to discrimination on the basis of dualism. The difference between this and discernment is that discrimination relies on a deflection of perception from reality as such, whereas discernment (and St Paul talks of the discernment of spirits) depends on the contemplation of reality by attention to reality and to the question addressed to reality: what is constructive and what is destructive in reality? What is constructive of life, of self, of relations to others and to the environment, and of a relationship to God, or destructive of all that? In the sense of evaluation, discernment judges so to speak on evidence, whereas discrimination prejudges, since it is a flight from reality. Discrimination is as it were the expression of a superego which obscures reality as it is; it considers reality to be subject to a law other than the actual law of reality (when we speak of the heteronomy of reality). It makes human beings themselves heteronomous, separating them from their autonomy, their own law, and their own judgement (discernment) of reality in their own reality. Discrimination replaces discernment with prejudice, whereas discernment discards discrimination on the basis of its freedom to contemplate reality and to evaluate it on evidence.

The challenge of Vatican II is to end an era of discrimination and to begin an era of discernment, of discernment of reality, out of awareness that God is the God of reality and faith, of faith in reality. For Roman Catholicism, this is tantamount to being summoned to undergo a kind of psychoanalysis in order to nominate and confront reality as that in and with and through which God meets us. Reality is the sign and instrument of God for the advent of faith and of the Church, which call for a correlation between reality and the Gospel, and more exactly the acknowledgement of the essential correlation between reality and the Gospel, and therefore discernment of this correlation. The Christian faith and Church call for awareness of this correlation, and are specifically and simultaneously the sign of its effectiveness and the instrument of its execution.

VII The integration of reality and recapitulation of everything in Christ

The ultimate challenge of Vatican II is the integration of reality. This is necessarily a critical integration, and an inclusion of reality at the cost of an exclusion. It cannot legitimately be a recovery of reality, which is a stranglehold on it and, as such, a resurgence of the Roman Catholic temptation to absolutism. Ultimately, integration cannot be the sole possession of any particular church or faith, since reality is God's reality and God is its sole master, just as the Church and its faith exist by him and for him and their master is the very master of reality. The critical integration of reality must pertain to God himself. That is the 'recapitulation' or consummation which the author of Ephesians says is the mystery of God's 'purpose, the hidden plan he so kindly made in Christ from the beginning to act upon when the times had run their course to the end, that he would bring everything together under Christ, as head, everything in the heavens and everything on earth' (Eph. 1.9–10).[2] He states that the ultimate intention of God's creative and redemptive plan is, as the standard French text says, *'récapituler'*: that is, literally, to give everything without exception a 'head' in Christ.[3] This is no plain statement of fact, the mere utterance of something that happens to be so, and which just has to be accepted purely and simply as being so, but a militant affirmation, testifying to something that is to come about and is confirmed only by happening. It is something that happens in a specific way and is significant in and for faith and for the Church, and with them and also through them, though not restrictively. The confirmation is inclusive and universal, but as an affirmation of faith which demands faith to be 'intelligible' and consciously, inwardly verifiable. The faith in question is faith in Christ, or in the threefold God, and that is the God who recapitulates, consummates, and brings everything together under Christ, as head.

This recapitulation consists in an assessment of reality, distinguishing in reality what is destructive and thus mortal from what is constructive and life-affirming: this assessment contains an exclusion and an inclusion, and turns what is excluded into matter for metamorphosis, a transformation, precisely by seeing it in the light of God the creator and redeemer, who always creates on the basis of nothing as such. Recapitulation also consists, through this dual, exclusive and inclusive, judgement, in the accomplishment of reality as reality in God, in the God who is the foundation of reality and also its end and goal. Faith and the Church can only draw from this recapitulation as from a vital spring and bear witness to it as the living source of reality as such. They do not have to, indeed cannot, carry out the recapitulation, but can signify it, fallibly as must be the case, but also trusting surely in the power of its advent, which will be stronger than themselves and their fallibility, and stronger too than the destructive aspect of reality.

Therefore Vatican II offers a threefold challenge as a Council of reconciliation, on behalf of an affirmation of faith in the invigorating power of Christ and therefore of faith in the consummation of everything in Christ. It calls for traditional Roman Catholicism to be removed from the impasse of an exclusivist and discriminatory theology; in other words, from delimitation. It calls for Roman Catholicism to be reconnected with reality as a whole by restoring the actual status of Catholicism and reality, which is for the truth of both to be manifested only through their relation or reference to Christ, or to God who recapitulates all things in Christ. It calls for Roman Catholicism, for its own sake and for that of reality as a whole, to be helped to open itself up to the process of consummation in Christ, and therefore to open up to the spiritual in order to discern the destructive–daemonic aspect in reality (including faith and Church), and to distinguish the constructive, angelic aspect from the daemonic.

There is yet another challenge to face: that of assisting the metamorphosis or transformation of the destructive void into constructive material, by highlighting the creative and redemptive power of God who accomplishes all things, 'who makes the dead live, and calls into being things that are not' (Rom. 4.17). When applied to the Roman Catholic Church, this means: assisting the passage through death of that which is fossilized and petrified, congealing and stupefying, so that it is transformed into vital energy and thus resurrected. This is the rebirth of the Roman Catholic Church, the work of Christ himself who remakes all things, transposing the Church from its former to its new state, and summoning the Church to follow the course of metamorphosis with deep confidence in Christ and in a state of profound love of human beings and of all reality, with courage, determination and patience.

The final challenge also implies the need to abandon the destructive forms of determinism which resist the process of consummation. There are diseases of faith linked to the abovementioned inimical temptations that lie unnoticed in near-obscurity. These sicknesses have to be diagnosed and identified before they can be treated, nursed and cured by the process of bringing to unity. In certain cases, sickness seems to masquerade as normality, which is a symptom of sectarian decline (the absolutization of one or other or of all the temptations of Roman Catholicism, which I have already described). Then, when all forms of treatment seem to fail, it is supremely tempting to attempt radical surgery and therefore excommunication. But it is prudent, and essential, to remember the lesson that multisecularism, and to date delimitation and therefore exclusion in that sense, is almost always counter-productive. This practice has surely always reduced the catholicity of the Roman Catholic Church, committing it to expend its energy in a contrary rather than a supportive campaign – supportive, that is, of Christ by whom all things are made new. Bringing to a head, and therefore judgement (exclusion and inclusion, inclusion at the cost of an exclusion) form part of this consummation in Christ. The correct reaction to the challenge in question is to invest in the health of faith and of the Church, by discerning in the decline (the sickness) in question the proportion of truth to be included, and by thus eroding from within the proportion of error that must be excluded. Either sickness is embraced and the old leaven remains, or it is purged out to make way for the new.

VIII Conclusion

Vatican II was the Roman Catholic Church's encounter with reality and with catholicity, the one inseparably implying the other. There is little point in asking whether this encounter was a success or a failure, and to what extent in either case. We too often look to the past, when there is a great risk of resorting to flight. The Church (which means the Roman Catholic Church like any other) has other, new encounters to experience with history and with God as the God of and in history. Reference to Vatican II is useful if it helps us to face these new encounters, but of little value if it deflects us from them. The new encounters apply to all the churches, and concern them all. The churches' only hope is to face them together in a truly conciliar effort. The appointment is always with reality and with catholicity. It always poses the question of the theology of delimitation *versus* the theology of recapitulation. It always poses the question of aptness to learn from the Creator Spirit.

This might be a petition to a future catholic pope,[4] upholding and upheld by the vital forces established in the Gospel of Christ (and therefore critically correlated with reality) and put to the test of one catholic faith and Church.

Amen: Veni Creator Spiritus. Come Holy Spirit, our souls inspire.

Translated by J. G. Cumming

Notes

1. The continuation of this article will be published later (*L'échéance–et le kairos–de Vatican II* and *La catholicité de Vatican II*). For date and place see the site http://www.premiumorange.com/theologie.protestante/gerardsiegwalt/pages/chrono.html.
2. Jerusalem Bible [Tr.].
3. Literally, to 'recapitulate everything in Christ' ('*anakephalaiomai*', Greek NT; '*instaurare omnia in Christo, quae in caelis, et quae in terra sunt, in ipso*', Vulgate; 'to bring everything to a unity in Christ', REB; 'to gather up all things in him', NRSV; 'all human history shall be consummated in Christ', Phillips; 'to bring everything together under Christ, as head', Jerusalem) [Tr.].
4. In Rome and elsewhere, since the seat of the apostles Peter and Paul (not to mention John and others) is where the spirit of Peter and Paul is to be found.

The 'Church of the Poor' did not Prosper at Vatican II

JON SOBRINO

The 'Church of the Poor' did not prosper at Vatican II. It was only when Medellín adopted it that essential elements in the Council became historical fact.

The summons that broke unexpectedly and radically with the past, the unprecedented freedom within the meeting itself and the relevance of many of its texts, quickly picked up by church people and those outside, transformed the Council into an epoch-making event. It caused an *impact,* which shook minds and consciences, and unleashed an *impulse* to create an updated Christianity that was more true to the Gospel. At the conceptual level, in a way the situation was ripe. But taking the Council as a whole, what was needed was an *irruption* or break-through, that did not derive from the dominant position, in fact at times was quite the contrary. Quiet in tone but with deep inner strength, the break-through occurred with the personality and behaviour of John XXIII. The Council opened the Church's windows and 'let in fresh air'. In Latin America, (for the most clear-sighted) it soon became a blessing.

However, the Church of the poor did not prosper, despite the explicit desires and words of John XXIII: 'Today the Church is above all the Church of the poor', he had said in a radio message.[1] Somewhat sadly, two months after the Council began, Cardinal Lercaro said: 'We all feel that the Council has been lacking something up till now.' He went on to repeat John XXIII's words: 'Today the Church is above all the Church of the poor.'[2] And Bishop Himmer of Tournai said categorically: *'primus locus in ecclesia pauperibus reservandus est'* (In the Church, the poor come first*)*.

In this article, I shall comment on three points. 1. The Church of the poor, which was mentioned at the Council, and emerged with force around

Medellín. 2. This Church recovered elements that were essential in the Council and made them become historical fact. 3. Archbishop Romero and Ignacio Ellacuría deepened the relationship between the Church and the poor by speaking of the *crucified people* and a *crucified Church,* which were not mentioned at the Council.

I The Church of the poor, the Council and the Catacombs Pact

1. The Church of the poor is a definite *gap* in the Council, which cannot be filled with texts, however important these may be for other chapters. 'In the poor and in those who are suffering the Church recognizes the image of its poor and suffering founder. It tries to meet their needs and to serve Christ in them' (*Lumen gentium:* LG 8). These words say something about the Church's mission and about spirituality, but they say nothing about the Church *being poor* or *being persecuted* for defending the poor. They did not take into account the historical and dialectic dimension of the poor, or their capacity to save. Yes, the Church must serve the poor, but the poor can also save the Church.

Something similar could be said about another well-known text: 'The joys and hopes, the sadness and distress...especially of the poor and those who are suffering, are the joys and hopes, the sadness and distress of the disciples of Christ' (*Gaudium et spes:* GS 1). These words express something that the Church must bear clearly in mind when it presents itself to the world. And by putting them at the beginning of *Gaudium et spes*, the Council showed how aware it was of their importance. And so it happened. Felix Wilfred says: 'There has been no other document so relevant for mission in Asia than *Gaudium et spes*'.[3] It sets believers on a creaturely level, but does not go beyond that, although it can be deepened through faith in Christ. But once again, the text does not say how the poor constitute the Church's *own self*.

2. Various bishops quickly grasped that the majority were far from seeing the Church as *devoted to the poor, in poverty and powerless, being poor herself*. In accordance with John XXIII's inspiration, these bishops met confidentially, regularly and without any sectarianism in *Domus Mariae* outside Rome. They thought deeply about 'the poverty of the Church' and a few days before the Council closed, about forty conciliar Fathers celebrated a Eucharist in the Catacombs of St Domitila.

They prayed that they might 'be faithful to the spirit of Jesus', and, when the celebration was over, they signed what they called the 'Catacombs Pact : a poor and servant Church'. The 'pact', one of whose proponents was Dom Helder Camara, was a challenge to their 'brother bishops' to lead a 'life of poverty' and to become a 'poor and servant' Church. The signatories (Latin Americans and from other continents) committed themselves to living in poverty, renouncing all the symbols and privileges of power and setting the poor at the centre of their pastoral ministry. The text, which was to have a strong influence at Medellín, begins thus: 'We, Bishops meeting at Vatican Council II, being aware of the deficiencies in our life of poverty according to the Gospel, encouraged by one another in this initiative, in which each one of us wants to avoid singularity and presumption...with humility and knowing our weakness, but also with full determination and all the strength God wants to give us as his grace, commit ourselves to the following:'

Then they list their commitment in 13 points, all to do with living 'in poverty and without power'.[4]

The idea and the commitment were taken up by Medellín in the chapter 'Poverty of the Church', in which the bishops examine their own poverty and that of their churches. And notably, they begin their reflections with two documents entitled 'Justice' and 'Peace'. These express the liberation that the Church must promote.

Then another fundamental thing happened. Unlike what happened at the Council, by making the poor and their necessary liberation central, Medellín had the economic, military and police powers and much of the media of the continent against it from the beginning. Remember the Rockefeller Report in 1969, the Santa Fe meeting document in 1980, the military meetings in the Southern Cone during the 1980s. Indeed, they unleashed cruel campaigns, which part of the institutional Church joined in. And this has recurred wherever the Church has remained faithful to Medellín. These were also times of martyrdom, the most Jesus-like in the Church.

The persecution frightened the institution, which also saw with fear how Medellín and various prominent bishops (as well as liberation theology) endowed Christians who defended the poor with *adulthood and freedom*. The institutional Church felt the power of the hierarchy was wobbling, which was seen to be a grave evil. And then came the reaction. Various bishops were abused, and liberation theology was fiercely opposed.

The Church of the poor became a reality. Ellacuría took a great theoretical step forward, with major practical consequences, when he stated the idea that 'the Church of the poor' must be understood as the Church in it, and not just as an option taken by the Church. An ethical focus is not enough. The Church of the poor 'is not one which stands outside the world of the poor, and generously offers them its help'.⁵ That is to say, the Church is not logically independent of the poor, so that it might ask itself – afterwards – what it should do with them. And this is not a 'regional' focus, as if the poor were just *part* of the Church.

The matter is theologically *fundamental*. 'The union of God with human beings, as it occurs in Jesus Christ, is historically a union of a God self-emptied primarily into the world of the poor'. The poor make up the Church from within. 'The poor are its principal subject and its internal structuring principle'. They permit and foster its *saving identity*. 'By becoming incarnate among the poor, ultimately dedicating its life to them and dying for them, the Church can establish itself in a Christian way as an effective sign of salvation for all people'.

Naturally and inescapably, the poor set the Church face to face with the Gospel. And when, as well as helping them, the Church defends them, then *ex opere operato* it confronts the idols, the *divinities* who bring death–a *theological* focus which brings final consequences: persecution and death. Then, of necessity, it becomes a *persecuted Church*, way beyond what was only stated generically at the Council: 'The Church walks in pilgrimage among the persecutions of the world and God's consolations' (LG 8).

It was not like that among us. Rutilio Grande said it with pastoral precision: 'It's dangerous to be a Christian in our midst. It's practically illegal...Because the world around us is rooted in an established *disorder*, in the face of which the mere proclamation of the Gospel is subversive (*Homily* of 13 February 1977). And in a passionate outburst, Archbishop Romero declared that persecution was a blessing: 'I am glad, brothers and sisters, that our Church should be persecuted, precisely for its preferential option for the poor, and for trying to become embodied in what concerns the poor' (15 July 1979).

The Council said nothing about *a Church crucified for the cause of justice*. These were not times to make the real poor and real crosses central to the Church – together with their Lord. But among us, the Church, with part of its hierarchy, confronted the anti-kingdom and became configured not only as a Church of the poor, but as a Church of the crucified. In another passionate outburst, Monsignor Romero said: 'It would be sad if in a country where there are so many horrible murders, we did not count priests among the victims. They are the testimony of a Church incarnate in the people's problems' (*Homily* of 24 June 1979).

The Council spoke of the poor but with restraint. Although the Council was not responsible, it was sad that with the backward march of the Vatican and other hierarchies, a studied insult was used to denigrate the 'Church of the poor' by calling it the 'popular Church'. The ploy was absurd, because there is nothing wrong with 'people' – popular – indeed much that is good. And it is a central concept in the Council, as well as in the Old and New Treatments. But there was no logic in their rejection of the Church of the poor, merely a determination to have done with that Church, the Church of Monsignor Romero, Don Samuel Ruiz, Leonidas Proaño...And to have done with liberation theology.

II Conciliar innovations empowered in the Church of the poor and becoming historical fact

Without the Council there would have been no Church of the poor, but it was not just the Council that brought it about. And without the Church of the poor, as it arose around Medellín, the Council would not have expanded its work of the Gospel so far in the Third World. Nor, in my opinion, would various fundamental elements of the Council have blossomed so creatively.

1. The Council returned to the *word of God: Dei verbum,* which had an important, lasting impact. It shaped the life of communities, religious life, theology and spirituality, what makes us live, personally and socially, in the sight of God and our fellow humans. The translation of biblical texts into the vernacular radically changed participation in the liturgy. The acceptance of literary genres helped people understand the meaning of the biblical texts in their historical context, and to go deeper into the history in whose light they should be read today. They ceased to be merely devotional texts.

All this was revolutionizing Christianity, because, if it is allowed to be, the Word of God is a sharp sword cutting to the quick. Obviously, with problems. The *fundamentalist* understanding of God's word persists, without setting it in its own time or letting it do its work in ours. So do the *Pentecostal* and the *integrist* forms of understanding in certain movements, *opus,* legionaries, heralds... In exaggeratedly devotional movements Scripture occupies second or third place. But to a large extent its importance is now irreversible.

In Latin America two very important things happened. There was an advance in classical hermeneutics: how to let the Scripture of yesterday speak today. From Carlos Mesters it was understood that the word of God speaks when (a) the text is (b) read in community, and (c) in actual occurring history. And there was also a fundamental identification of the Church 'of the poor' with 'the poor and oppressed', who are central to the prophets and to Jesus.

2. The Council recovered the *people of God*. The Church is not an ecstatic society but a 'people', who have to walk amidst the ups and downs of history, accompanying God and accompanied by God. Being a 'people' in this way, is not sociology – Ratzinger's bugbear – but goes to the heart of faith: to *walk* humbly with God (Micah 6.8), to *follow* Jesus (Mark 8.34). And it is incumbent upon it to be inserted into the social reality, which in Latin America means a reality of the poor and oppressed. Not, basically, to belong ethnically to a race or historico-culturally to a *Volk*. Thus 'people' expresses better the social sin of some and the liberating struggles and hopes of others.

Being a 'people' manifests a *democratic principle*, arousing fear and suspicion in the hierarchy. In the Church of the poor what being a 'people' manifests is *the principle of life, solidarity, dignity*.

3. The Council called for *'discerning the signs of the times'*. A sensible demand since it is difficult to serve the world (as the General Congregation of the Society of Jesus, GC 3, asks) without knowing it well. They are *signs of the times* in the historico-pastoral sense (GS 4). This required an act of humility, because it suggested that for centuries the Church had not felt the need to look at the world in order to know what it ought to do. And, as an even greater surprise, the Council added that we should discern in history 'the true signs of God's presence or plans'. They are the *signs* in the historico-theological sense (GS 11). Without scrutinizing the signs of the times no proper *aggiornamento* is possible. And as we scan them, although we must always walk 'contending with God', for of course we may meet God along the way.

Medellín took very seriously the need to scan the signs of the times. But something happened there which had not happened at the Council: the poor 'broke through' and with them God 'broke through'.[6] This means that, with logical and chronological precedence, *grasping* the break-through comes before *discerning* it. And more important than sharpening a blurred vision is overcoming *blindness in the face of the obvious*.

4. The Council thought of the universal Church also as *communio*, which Ratzinger made theologically absolute. What arose, in fact, were 'little communities', 'base' communities, as Karl Rahner comments, so that the Spirit may blow from the valley and not from the heights, and in order to live the faith in a more personal way. In the Church of the poor the fundamental thing is that the base is the poor, 'and that only the poor in community can avoid both excessive institutionalization and secularization.'[7] That is why Ellacuría said that the important thing about the base communities is that they should really be 'basic', sharing in real poverty, living, suffering and celebrating there, addressing God from there, with their whole burden of poverty and often with wings given by the spirit. Then they become 'communities of the poor with spirit'.

5. *Collegiality* was important at the Council, although it suffered ups and downs and could not overcome the pyramidal structure of a hierarchical Church. At Medellín, the idea prospered at two levels. At the formal level, it was bolstered by the Latin American Bishops' Council (CELAM), which organized Medellín and Puebla. These took place before (and more fruitfully) than in other continents. Collegiality also prospered at the more historical level, with the awareness of another *college:* that of the so-called 'Fathers of the Church of Latin America'.[8] Some of these, like Dom Helder, were present at the Council. Others joined after the Council. And above all, what drove them to become a *college* was the suffering reality of the poor. All of them had in common a total dedication to the poor–the indigenous; some were persecuted for this cause and some of them were murdered together with their people.

The Council's contribution was not to have held back the creativity of those bishops who went beyond, and sometimes in the opposite direction to, the Vatican curia. A distinguished example was Monsignor Romero who, in his archdiocese, also set up a vigorous ecclesial *body* consisting of all its men and women, which was *collegial* in the primary gospel sense.

III Beyond the Council and without support. 'The crucified people'

The Council spoke of the 'people' of God, but its theology did enter into this people's historical reality. But that is what happened so boldly among us.

Both Archbishop Romero and Ignacio Ellacuría understood the

collective people–peasants, oppressed, repressed – as *crucified*. Ellacuría formulated it expressly as the 'crucified people'. Monsignor Romero said it very effectively by implication: 'I denounce wealth, private property, as an untouchable absolute...Woe to anyone who touches this high tension wire! He gets burnt!' (12 August 1979). 'They manipulate multitudes because they keep many people down by hunger (16 December 1979). 'I will never tire of denouncing the outrage of arbitrary arrests, disappearances, torture' (24 June 1979). 'Violence, murder, torture where there are so many dead, cutting people up and throwing them into the sea, dumping bodies: this is the reign of hell' (1 July 1979).

Monsignor Romero compared them to *Christ* crucified on 19 June 1977 in Aguilares, after a month of murders of peasants: 'You are the image of the Pierced Divine One... [This people] is the image of all people who, like the people in Aguilares, are attacked and abused'. In a text written in preparation for Puebla in 1978, Ellacuría created and consecrated the expression 'crucified people' and compared it to Yahweh's 'suffering servant'. This was not based on the Council or on tradition.

For both of them, the term *people* has a historical, social, economic, dialectical and confrontational reality and so does this people's destiny: *crucifixion*. Crucified people and people of God may converge in reality. In the Council *texts* the term *people* is less historic, whereas in the texts cited above, it is radically historical. The *crucified people* points to Jesus crucified, and thus christologizes the people, taking a further leap than that taken by the Council when it ecclesiologized them.

Archbishop Romero, a clear-sighted pastor, gave the crucified people an insuperable vigour. Ellacuría, a pastoral intellectual, gave them rigorous conceptual precision. And for that he also made use of an important conciliar category, and broadened it unexpectedly: the 'signs of the times'. He wrote: 'Among all the signs, some conspicuous and others barely perceptible, which always exist in every period, there is one that is the main sign, in whose light the others need to be seen and interpreted. This sign is always the historically crucified people, which as well as being constant, always takes a different historical form of crucifixion. This people is the historical continuation of the Servant of Yahweh.'[9]

1. 'Signs of the times' is usually used to point out new *positive* realities, but in Ellacuría's text it expresses a totally *negative* reality: the '*crucified* people'. This stubborn insistence on the negative aspect of history is not common, especially in 'light' periods like the present.

2. The crucified people is *the* principal sign among others, some visible and some barely perceptible. And in its light 'all the others must be understood'. So it is a reality that also functions as a hermeneutical principle to understand the whole of reality.

3. It is 'always' this principal sign. It is important to remember that because history makes it impossible to conceal. There continue to be peoples who are preyed on as in the Congo, ignored as in Haiti, devastated by a murder epidemic like the Central Americans.

4. Finally, the crucified people 'brings salvation'; it is the suffering servant of the songs in Isaiah, the crucified Jesus of the gospels.

This is Ellacuría's most original contribution, which I cannot dwell on here. We may simply recall the title of his 1978 article: 'The Crucified People. An Essay in *Historical Soteriology*'. This people brings salvation, because being a product of our own hands, it gives us access to our own truth, which is no small salvation. It has human values, not so common in other places: welcome, simplicity, sharing. With spirit it organizes and work for liberation. And, above all, these individuals want to live together with one another. This is what we have called *primordial holiness*. With them the liberating and crucified God passes through our world.

This crucified people, saving and believing, is the greatest expression of the Church of the poor.

The impulse of Vatican II culminated in Medellín, but Medellín was more than the mere application or extrapolation of the Council. At the Council, there was a lesser break-through in the subjective sphere of hopes and theologies. At Medellín, there was a more powerful break-through in the *objective* sphere: the poor, their oppression and their real faith and hope.

At the Council, there was an impulse not to be ashamed of the modern world and to use the modern to make the Christian God more credible. At Medellín, there was an impulse not to be ashamed of the poor and no longer to hear the biblical reproach: 'Because of you God's name is blasphemed among the nations.' And with humility, it set to work to 'wash God's face'.

Translated by Dinah Livingstone

Notes

1. 11 September 1962.
2. 6 December 1962.
3. F. Wilfred, 'The Reception of Vatican II in a Multi-Religious Continent' (in this issue of *Concilium*).

4. The text can be seen in *Carta a las Iglesias* San Salvador, 590 (June 2009), pp. 6–8.
5. This and the following three quotations are taken from 'La Iglesia de los pobres, Sacramento hístorico de liberación', *Estudios Centroamericanos* (ECA) (a San Salvador periodical) (November–December 1977), p. 717.
6. On the expression 'break-through' see my article 'Recuperar y poner a producir a Jesús de Nazareth y su cruz en un mundo de pobres y oprimido', *Revista Latinoamericana de Teología,* 82 (2011), pp. 49–51.
7. *Ibid.*
8. See *Fathers of the Church in Latin America*, the monographic issue of *Concilium* (2009) 5.
9. 'Discernir los signos de los tiempos', *Diakonia*, 18 (1981), p. 58.

The Council and the Emergence of the Laity

MARIA CLARA LUCCHETTI BINGEMER

The celebration of the fiftieth anniversary of the Council invites to look again at this important event. Elected Pope in 1958, John XXIII surprised the world by calling the Council. His aim was to rethink and renew the customs of Christian people and adapt Church discipline to the conditions of the modern world. The Italian word *aggiornamento* came to express what the Council wanted and the results it desired and worked for.

In John XXIII's prophetic vision, the Council was to be a sort of 'new Pentecost', that is, a deep and wide-ranging experience that would reconstitute the Catholic Church, not just as an institution, but also as a dynamic gospel movement, imbued with openness and renewal. This was the beginning of the process that resulted in the Second Vatican Council and which was like the 'breeze heralding an unexpected spring', in the Pope's own words. Its characteristics were openness and a desire for reconciliation with the world in all its complexity.

Whereas previous Councils had had as their main concern to condemn heresies, define truths of faith and correct errors that obscured the full light of truth, Vatican II from the beginning was directed essentially at looking for a more positive and participatory role for the Catholic faith in society. It wanted not just to discuss dogmatic theological definitions, but also to turn its attention to social and economic problems, seeing them not as threats, but as genuine pastoral challenges demanding a response from the Church.

In defining the nature of the Council he was calling, John XXIII declared emphatically, with pastoral firmness and courage, that he did not want to make yet another list of errors and condemnations, as had happened so often in the past. What he wanted was for the Church to show more mercy and less severity. In his view, this would be a better reply to the needs of the day and would also give the Church a more maternal and welcoming appearance.

The question of the laity who wanted greater participation in the Church's life and mission was one of the important points the Council dealt with. It set the seal on the emergence of the laity in the Church and the acceptance by the Church's magisterium of a theology of the laity that had already been developed by great European theologians.[1] The Council documents themselves are full of reflections on the laity and statements about their importance to the Church today.[2]

This article will examine some of the most important documents dealing with these questions and revisit the challenges they pose for theology today. By the end of the article, I hope to have raised some points born under the renewing breeze of the Council but which now face the challenge of going beyond the Council itself.

I Back to the sources

The Council speaks a lot about the laity, and very positively. The apostolic lay movements that had been very active in the decades before the Council gave the Council fathers valuable material that enabled them to move forward, despite the obstacles, towards an ecclesiology that was more integrated and structured by communion.[3]

In this way, the Council sought to overcome, at least in part, the definition of the laity in negative terms (not priest, not monk, not a Religious), emphasizing a more positive characterization (member of the People of God through baptism) and valuing them as active members, responsible for building up the fabric of the Church.[4]

1. It proclaims and consecrates a definition of the Church in which the common Christian state is prior to the diversity of functions, gifts and ministries. The Constitution on the Church, *Lumen gentium*, presents the Church community as the People of God, in which all are full members.[5]

2. It gives new value to community, in contrast to the vertical and hierarchizing ecclesiologies that Yves Congar called 'hierarchologies'.[6]

What is vital for the self-understanding of the Christian layperson within the church community is the Council's attitude in this document, when it declares that the laity are not subjects or mere servants of the pastors but their sisters and brothers: 'As the laity through the divine choice have Christ as their brother, who, though Lord of all, came not to be served but to serve (cf Mt 20.28), they also have as brothers those in the sacred ministry who by teaching, by sanctifying and by ruling with the authority of Christ so nourish the family of God that the new commandment of love may be fulfilled by all.'[7]

In so doing, the Council recovered important constitutive elements of what had been the Church's self-understanding from the earliest times. The New Testament, when it tried to describe the structure of Christ's Church, did not make use of the concept of 'layperson' or something equivalent to the existing laity of today; on the contrary, we find that this concept is absent.[8] It prefers to talk about disciples, Christians, faithful, believers, the elect, or saints, without singling them out as lay and non-ordained.

Nor is Jesus himself presented as a priest. He is what would be called today a 'secular' person, with no specific power or ministry in the official religion, indeed someone who questions the established religious power in the institution of his religion.[9] This situation is fully accepted by the Christians of his time and subsequent centuries.[10]

On the contrary, throughout the pages of the New Testament we find that the diversity of ministries exists from the beginning. When mentioning the gifts and services in the People of God, the New Testament text stresses that there is one Spirit, but various gifts and ministries that flow from him (cf. 1 Cor. 12). At the same time as this diversity is affirmed, it seems clear that for Jesus the group of the Twelve is particularly important (Acts 1.21–2) and that he treats them differently from the way he treats the rest of the disciples, and entrusts them with different missions. It is therefore wrong to say that the Church in its beginnings lacked any organization and operated in enthusiastic anarchy, with its eyes fixed on the imminent Parousia.

Nevertheless, despite the existence of this structured community and the distribution of services, for the churches of the New Testament the whole people of God (*laos*) is consecrated and priestly, and the idea of 'church' stresses this, being the congregational and assembled dimension of the community of believers.[11] Within this church body, the minister continues to be one of the baptized, a disciple of Jesus. He does not form a separate group with his peers, but shares in the common Christian dignity, even though he has specific functions proper to his ministry. In this sense, every Christian is anointed by the Spirit and there are no groups of specialists or privileged people, separate from the majority of the faithful.[12]

But if God has one people, not all are ministers. How can ministers be distinguished from others? Certainly Christianity suffered the influence of the pre-Christian conceptions that dominated Graeco-Roman culture, in which *laos* meant the people in the sense of plebs, a rather pejorative term, with the implication of uneducated, coarse, illiterate, primitive, and so on. As they expanded across the then known world, the first communities to some extent incorporated this view and gradually absorbed the idea of the 'ordinary Christian' with a connotation of subordination and passivity. This was a person who allowed himself or herself to be guided, who is taught and led by another person who knows, is active and governs. This made it difficult to maintain the sense of the common Christian dignity between those who are ordained ministers and those who are not.[13]

The evolution of the term and the concept led to the layperson being seen in two dimensions: *theologically*, as a Christian without any other adjectives, since the earliest days of Christianity, and *sociologically*, as the Christian who is not a minister, from the second and third centuries onwards.

Such ambiguities were encountered and overcome by Augustine of Hippo, who in the fourth century made this statement about his Episcopal mission: 'What I am for you terrifies me, but being with you consoles me. I am for you as a bishop; I am with you as a Christian. The first names an office, the second, a grace; one means risk, the other salvation.'[14] The result was a move in the direction of a 'dichotomous confusion', which the Council faced and sought to resolve.

The conciliar Fathers realized, with the help of the theologians who advised them, that this dichotomy falsified the New Testament revelation. According to the New Testament, all the members of the Church are priests, because they share in the one priesthood of Christ. The origin of the later dichotomies lies, in fact, in dualisms foreign to the authentic Christian experience.[15]

The theological and ecclesial consequences of this state of affairs are serious:

1. A downgrading of the common priesthood of the faithful and a diminution of the importance of baptism as compared with the consecration conferred in the sacrament of order and religious vows;

2. A downplaying of the dignity of baptized Christians as compared with the ordained ministers;

3. An assumption of subordination and passivity in baptized Christians' understanding of their responsibility for the Church's mission;

4. A distorted view that identifies the cleric with the educated, the scholar, and the layperson with the uneducated, the idiot who cannot read the Scriptures and so has no share in decision-making in the Church.[16]

Lumen gentium, however, restores the base that is the foundation of everything and on which the Church can be built, baptism, the common ground of belonging to Christ and which makes all Christians together the People of God. Only subsequently is this concept expanded into specific ministries, according to the gifts the Spirit distributes in the community.

II The mission of the laity

When it starts to define the layperson, the Council takes as its basis his or her secularity.[17] The layperson is the man or woman who has to build the human city and deal with what is profane, leaving the sacred to the clergy and the religious.

In the conciliar documents – and in a special way in *Lumen gentium* – two ecclesiologies coexist, one juridical and one based on communion.[18] Although the second of these was given priority over the first, the fact that the two coexist has a marked influence on other related ecclesiological topics. The topic of the laity in the Church is one of these.

In Chapter 4 of *Lumen gentium*, paragraph 31, the Council understands by the term 'laity' 'all the faithful except those in Holy Orders and those who belong to a religious state approved by the Church'. Although the definition begins positively ('all the faithful'), and the Constitution affirms the fundamental equality of all the baptized within the people of God, the continuation takes a juridical line and includes a negative slant: the layperson is still the non-cleric, the non-religious, the person who has not been given some 'special' gift or vocation or ministry in the Church.

This has an impact on the understanding of the mission of the laity. We certainly have the affirmation in the definition, in the same paragraph (31): 'Their secular character is proper and peculiar to the laity.' While clerics are said to engage in secular activities or professions 'sometimes', 'yet by reason of their particular vocation, they are principally and expressly ordained to the sacred ministry', the apostolic ministry of the laity is clearly situated in the world.

In saying this, *Lumen gentium* 31 opens up a positive perspective in recognizing the work of this majority part of the People of God, but subtly reinforces the dichotomy between religious and secular, between the Church and the present world, in the way it conceives of the Church.

When discussing the apostolate of the laity, *Apostolicam actuositatem* also stresses its secular character: 'The characteristic of the lay state being a life lived in the midst of the world and of secular affairs, laypeople are called by God to make of their apostolate, through the vigour of their Christian spirit, a leaven in the world.'[19] As a result, their Christian formation must be designed for this purpose: 'In this way laypeople actively insert themselves deeply into the very reality of the temporal order and take their part competently in the work of the world. At the same time, as living members and witnesses of the Church, they bring its presence and action into the heart of the temporal sphere.'[20]

And the laity's areas of apostolic action should also be predominantly in the secular sphere. The Decree mentions 'Church communities, the family, the young, the social environment, national and international spheres'.[21] Nevertheless, according to *Apostolicam actuositatem*, the laity should also work in the Church. Paragraph 10 describes this work in positive terms, though it emphasizes the participation of the faithful especially in the material and organizational aspects of the Church's life: the administration of goods, material and human resources. Among strictly pastoral activities, only catechesis is explicitly mentioned as the field of communicating the Word of God proper to the laity.[22]

III Assimilating the Council to take it further

This vision has brought undeniable advances, not just for the laity, but for the whole Church. It has restored the dignity of the laity by giving them official status as part of the ecclesial body. It has moved lay Christians from their status as mere spectators of a pastoral ministry organized by the hierarchy to being participants in it.

Nevertheless, in my view, the dichotomy that permeates the conciliar documents on the question of the secular character of the lay state still affects the structure of the Church community as regards its composition and formation, and this is rooted in a core dichotomy, the distinction *clergy–laity*, associated with which there is another: *religious–non-religious*. The first refers to the difference of essence (not degree) between the common priesthood of the faithful and the hierarchical priesthood, the second to the structure of the Church based on different states of life, but directed to the common goal of the universal call to holiness.

This twofold distinction gives rise to a third, the distinction *sacred–temporal* or *sacred–profane*. It divides the first distinction into two 'functional' groups: the laity are responsible for looking after the temporal and material sphere (family, social structures, politics). This is their field. In turn, the clergy and the religious deal with the things of the spirit, the sacred. They perform, administer and distribute the sacraments and symbolic 'resources' on which the community lives and is nourished. And the religious bear witness in the world to the spirit of the beatitudes.[23]

There can be increasingly seen today, especially in some recent trends in theology,[24] an attempt to resolve these distinctions. Do they not, it is asked, impoverish the breadth of spirit of a conciliar ecclesiology based on the over-arching category of the People of God? They do, indeed, seem to derive from the other ecclesiology that also runs through the conciliar documents, one that is more juridical and hierarchical.

These new theologies suggest that the distinctions can be resolved by setting up a new axis of dialectical tension: community <——> gifts/ministries. This would restore the Church's vocation as an inclusive baptismal community in which the gifts are received and the ministries exercised as forms of service.[25]

The effect of these new theologies (which seek to recover the true spirit of the Council) is to take to the ultimate consequences the primacy of the ontology of grace over any other possible distinction. The pneumatological dimension of the Church comes first. The Holy Spirit acts on the whole community and calls forth the different gifts to build up the Body of Christ. Ministerial status belongs to the whole Church and not to some sectors of it. Even the categories 'layperson' and 'laity' are left behind and exist only as negative abstractions that impoverish the dynamism of the Church.

The ecclesiology that emerges from this is a 'total ecclesiology',[26] and 'laicity' is a dimension of the whole Church present in history. The words 'layperson' and 'laity', in this view, gradually, and before very long, lose their purpose and fade away. Awakened by the Council, the laity's sense of themselves gradually evolves until it becomes an awareness of full citizenship and responsibility for the church community in the service of the project of the Kingdom of God announced by Jesus.

This whole course of theological reflection on the topic of the laity in the last fifty years today raises some challenging questions:

1. In the first centuries of Christian experience, the Church as a whole was seen as offering the world an alternative. The distinction was not between 'spiritual specialists' and 'Christians devoted to temporal affairs', but between the new vision of Christianity and the society that was to be evangelized. The Church of the first period also does not seem to show any signs of the current phenomenon of the laity, but thinks of itself as all the baptized. Can we therefore say that for us today there is an urgent need to 'go back to the sources' to rediscover the roots of what we today call 'laypeople' and the 'laity'?

2. The new theological tendencies seem to suggest the gradual elimination of the division inherent in the category 'layperson' in favour of a new, more inclusive ecclesiology, completely generated by the Spirit and ministerial in character, without dichotomies and distinctions. Nevertheless, underneath the seductively positive appearance of this theory, there remains a suspicion: isn't abolishing the word avoiding the problem? Behind this tendency may there not lie the risk of a new sort of clericalization, in which diluting the specific character of the laity may mean an attempt to camouflage and leave untouched the thorny and delicate issue of power in the Church? In short, may it not mean trying to reach a synthesis without having undergone and assimilated the antithesis represented by the uncomfortable reality of the distinction that still exists between the *teaching Church* and the *learning Church*?

IV Conclusion: trying out a new paradigm for post-conciliar times

As a result of the movement initiated by the Council, there have been a number of notable achievements by laypeople that seem to point towards a new paradigm. By necessity or force of circumstance, laypeople have been taking on and exercising ministries and services previously restricted to clergy or religious and as a result of this process models are emerging that seem to point to a new paradigm of the lay state. These models are inspired by the conciliar renewal, but represent bold steps beyond it.

1. *Lay theologians, men and women*. In a Church in which priestly and religious vocations have diminished dramatically, theological institutes and theology courses today often find that the majority of their students and teachers are laypeople. Disproving the criticisms of eminent theologians, such as Hans Urs von Balthasar, that these laypeople were really frustrated

priests who undertook theological training in order to exercise an unfulfilled vocation, the number of lay theologians (especially women) is constantly increasing.[27] Many do valuable service to reflection on the faith and venture into controversial topics that they know from experience and on which they can make expert and solidly-based contributions. Lay people today seek and obtain academic qualifications in the best institutes and faculties all round the world. They are thus qualified to teach in any academic institution on an equal footing with priests or religious.[28]

2. *Spiritual directors*: In earlier periods it was common to find an 'older' person, or someone more experienced, who accompanied others in their journeys in prayer and spirituality. This person could be a layperson or a priest. Subsequently this role became more restricted to priests, partly because it was (wrongly) identified with the sacrament of confession.

Today, however, countless laypeople, men and women, are taking on this role: they preach retreats, accompany people and produce prayer and liturgical material at various levels. Remarkable results are being achieved by these spiritual directors, who help so many people in the following of Jesus Christ and listening to the Spirit.

3. *Liturgy coordinators*: Among other things, the Council's liturgical reform succeeded in giving laypeople not just passive, 'consumer' roles, but also more active, 'producer' roles. It is well-known that women have had the predominant role here, creating liturgical spaces and events in which the People of God are able to express their faith with joy and beauty, faithful to the tradition, but also free in the Spirit's endless creativity.

This new paradigm that these men and women have developed is a rich and mature fruit brought by the conciliar renewal that today seeks to expand until it reaches its full potential.

Translated by Francis McDonagh

Notes

1. The greatest of these was Yves Congar, with his monumental work *Lay People in the Church*, London, 1959.
2. See especially chapter 4 of the *Dogmatic Constitution on the Church*, *Lumen gentium* (LG) and the *Decree on the Laity*, *Apostolicam actuositatem* (AA). (The English versions of the Council documents are taken from A. Flannery (ed.), Vatican Council II, *The Conciliar and Post-Conciliar Documents*, Wilmington, DE, 1975, adapted to inclusive language where necessary. Tr.).
3. Especially Action Catholique, started in France by Fr Lebret, which became enormously

important. V. A. J. de Almeida, *Leigos em que? Uma abordagem histórica*, São Paulo, Paulinas, 2006, esp. chapter 19, pp. 249–68
4. LG 30
5. LG 31
6. Cf. Y. Congar, *op. cit.*
7. LG 32
8. On this see my article 'O Batismo fonte do ministério cristão: o caso das CEBs' *Concilium* (Brazil), 334 (2010), pp. 35–47.
9. Cf. John 8, also Matt. 21.12–4; Mark 11.11–5; Luke19.45–7; John 2.13–21.
10. Cf. J. Estrada Díaz, *La identidad de los laicos. Ensayo de eclesiologia*, Madrid, 1990, p. 18. In any case, the constant view of New Testament exegesis has been that only Jesus truly merits the title of priest. On this, cf S. Galimberti and E. Malnatti, *Il cristiano nella storia oggi*, Trieste, 1994, p. 83. Cf also A. Faivre, *Les laics aux origines de l'Église*, Paris, 1984.
11. Cf. S. Galimberti & E. Malnatti, *op. Cit.*, p. 84.
12. Cf. *Ibid.*, p. 117: 'What is typical of Christianity is that all are consecrated to God, that there is no Christian who has a profane life.'
13. Cf what Yves Congar says about this in his book *Pour une église servante et pauvre*, Paris, 1963. See also M. Guerra, *Teología del sacerdocio* IV, Burgos, 1972, quoted in J. Estrada Díaz, *op. cit.*, p. 117, n. 8.
14. St Augustine, Serm. 340, 1 (Migne, PL 38, 1483), quoted in LG 32.
15. Cf. S. Galimberti & E. Malnatti, *op. cit.*, p. 99.
16. On all this, in addition to the authors already mentioned, cf. A. J de Almeida, *op. cit.*, especially Chapter 7, pp. 101–15.
17. LG 33, 35, 36; *Gaudium et spes* 43; AA 2; 29
18. On this, see A. Acerbi, *Due Ecclesiologie: Ecclesiogia giuridica ed Ecclesiologia di comunione nella LG*, Bologna, 1975.
19. AA 2.
20. AA 29.
21. AA 9.
22. This is a field of action traditionally entrusted to the laity, especially women.
23. Cf. LG 31.
24. See especially B. Forte, *La chiesa, icono della Trinitá: breve ecclesiologia*, Brescia, 1984, as well as the previously mentioned works by A. J. de Almeida and J. Estrada Díaz, and in addition the work of S. Dianich, E. Schillebeeckx, etc. In contrast, the way of resolving the dichotomy suggested here comes from earlier on, from Congar himself, who, in *Ministères et Communion Écclesiale* (Paris, 1971), goes further than he did in *Lay People in the Church*.
25. Cf. B. Forte, *op. cit.*, pp. 32–3.
26. The term comes from B. Forte, *op. cit.*
27. Cf. H. U. von Balthasar, *New Elucidations*, San Francisco, 1986, especially the chapter entitled 'A note on lay theologians' (pp. 198ff).
28. It is nevertheless the case (as I sadly know from experience) that often they are not admitted to positions that they could occupy with distinction and dedication.

Part Two: Theological Forum

Look Back to the Future
Transformative Impulses of Vatican II for African Catholicism

AGBONKHIANMEGHE E. OROBATOR, SJ

A recent account of what happened at the Second Vatican Council recalls the term *aggiornamento* ('bringing up to date') 'as a shorthand expression . . . to describe what the Council was about'.[1] Rare are the African languages that translate *aggiornamento* or render its variant meaning in their vocabulary. This observation supports the view that Vatican II bypassed Africa. Judging by the small number of indigenous bishops, the 'presence of Africa at Vatican II was marginal and by proxy'; thus, 'Africa had little effect on Vatican II itself'.[2] Understandably, compared to the optimism generated in the West, Christians in Africa 'have not felt the same affinity with the Council'.[3] Paradoxically, however, the intervening years have witnessed a phenomenal growth of African Catholicism in ways that 'may well have become possible only because of the changes initiated by the Council'.[4] Vatican II generated momentous impulses not for updating or renewal (for the Church in Africa was still 'a newborn community trying to find its place in a fast-moving continent'[5]) but for the growth of Catholicism in Africa.

I Historical context

At the cusp of Pope John XXIII's historic convocation of Vatican II, Africa swirled in a vortex of historical turbulence, political revolution, and religious transformation. Three events illustrate the thrust of this vortex. First, in reaction to the oppressive European colonialism that 'had carved up large chunks of Africa' in the service of Western economic and political interests,[6] Africa experienced an effervescence of nationalism and political emancipation. Not unlike African churches, new nations were emerging from the dying embers of colonialism. Second, similarly, albeit of a different order, African theology was tracing and defining the contours of its identity in the context of indigenous cultures and religions. Third, directly related to the second factor, churches in Africa were interrogating their parent bodies in view of acquiring autonomy, selfhood, and self-reliance.[7] These historical events define the context of the impulses generated by Vatican II for the mission and nature of the Church in Africa, the growth of African Catholicism, the development of African theology, and the inculturation of Catholicism in Africa.

II Ecclesiology, theology, inculturation and Catholicism in Africa since Vatican II

Laurenti Magesa has observed that 'perhaps the most important consequence of Vatican II for African Catholicism was the convocation in 1994 of the Special Assembly of the Synod of Bishops for Africa or African Synod, almost three decades after the closing of the Council'.[8] Almost 50 years later, a second African Synod took place in Rome. The combination of synodal assemblies confirms the maturation and self-confidence of African Catholicism. Characteristically, this development is represented in demographic and statistical terms that indicate an exponential growth of African Catholicism from just nine per cent of the population in 1910 to 63 per cent in 2010.[9] The vitality of African Catholicism since Vatican II is quantifiable not only in numbers but more in terms of its position as a critical partner in the Third Church and a key player in shaping the next Christendom.[10] The issues that African Catholicism brings to the table strain traditional categories and open up new directions in the tradition of Vatican II's *aggiornamento*.[11]

Since Vatican II, the Church in Africa has discovered its public role, vocation, and mission in the socio-economic and political arena. This consciousness shows in the outcomes of the second African Synod (2009) that identified the Church in Africa as agent of reconciliation, justice, and peace.[12] A similar process has occurred in the theological self-understanding of the Church. The first African Synod contextualized Vatican II's ecclesiology of the 'people of God' as the 'family of God', understood as the new way of being church in Africa. It must be said that 'To the African Church the idea ("people of God") was not really new. The people never had known anything else in their experience'.[13] Yet one of the unfulfilled impetuses of Vatican II is the potential of the African Church to shed its dependence on the Western Church for material and financial sustenance. The lack of progress in this area indicates that 'the Catholic Church in Africa is clearly under colonial administration'.[14]

African theology emerged in difficult circumstances. The debate about the principle, necessity, and validity of *'une théologie de couleur africaine'*[15] predates Vatican II; but, 'the outward-looking decrees of Vatican II itself, of course, gave a new impetus to this movement....'[16] On the eve of the Council, Eurocentric theologians argued against African theology as a legitimate branch of theological scholarship.[17] That would change when, first, in the wake of Vatican II's *Ad gentes,* Pope Paul VI rallied the African Church with a clarion call: '... you may, and you must, have an African Christianity'; and, second, Pope John Paul II used the term 'African theology' publicly on 9 April 1985.

The emergence and development of African theology happened in the context of African religion. Although Vatican II does not mention African religion by name, by virtue of its *Declaration on the Relationship of the Church to Non-Christian Religions (Nostra aetate),* the Council 'slightly opened the door for consideration of African religion as a dialogue'.[18] This implied the recognition of African religious traditions as a valid context for the salvific activity of the risen Christ and a fertile soil for the implantation of the Church of Christ (*Nostra aetate* 2–3; *Ad gentes* 6; *Lumen gentium* 16).[19] In this sense, 'Vatican II's openness and tolerance toward various cultures and religions may be its most important contribution to the Church in Africa'.[20] In the light of the foregoing, inculturation represents one of the impetuses of Vatican II for the growth of Catholicism and the development of theology in Africa.[21] Although Vatican II's *Sacrosanctum concilium* was initially interpreted and confined to the adaptation of liturgical symbols and practices,[22] in time it has come to be understood as a radical transformation of the whole life of the Church in the light of the Gospel. The Council prompted liturgical creativity and experimentation drawing on 'the spiritual adornments and gifts' of African cultures (*Sacrosanctum concilium* 37). Examples abound of liturgical rites that employ rich symbolisms of African cultures and religious traditions.[23] Yet, there are attempts to impose limits on the scope of Paul VI's idea of an African Christianity and, thus, reverse the movement of liturgical creativity and renewal stimulated by Vatican II. Ecclesiastical and bureaucratic control means that the score sheet of liturgical inculturation 'remains unimpressive'.[24] According to Magesa, 'currently, in view of Roman systematic centralization after the centrifugal phenomenon spearheaded by Vatican II, it is becoming more difficult for an initiative of this kind even to be submitted to Rome: many bishops are either afraid or embarrassed to do so'.[25]

III   Vatican III: 'Look to the future without fear'[26]

Africa's theological memory of Vatican II is sparse, pithy, and uneventful. Notwithstanding Karl Rahner's glowing assessment of Vatican II as an epoch-making 'first assembly of the world-episcopate',[27] history shows that at this 'Council of the world-Church', 'only sporadic voices were heard from Africa'.[28] The largely expatriate African episcopate 'dealt only with matters internal to their Churches: liturgical and, above all, canonical and disciplinary issues'.[29] In the intervening years, as the hitherto unquestioned fusion of Christianity and the West has collapsed, vibrant and dynamic new voices have emerged outside the traditional historical enclaves of Catholicism.

The southward shift of global Catholicism means that the 'joys and hopes; pain and anguish' of African Catholicism are no longer peripheral to world Catholicism. The former delineates a new ecclesial context that generates an acute consciousness of new concerns and challenges, such as the participation of women in ecclesial ministry and leadership; the place of 'the grief and anguish… of the poor and afflicted' in the missiological purview of the global church; the escalating threat of militant Islam; globalization and its attendant cultural, economic, and political consequences; the quest for ecclesial autonomy; ethnic rivalry; systemic corruption; and multi-directional flows of migrants and forcibly-displaced peoples. To respond to these challenges and offer credible answers to these questions, the African Church not only needs to 'look back on the Council to seek guidance';[30] also, more importantly, it looks to a future Third Vatican Council, spearheaded by the Third Church, to generate a 'new Pentecost' of renewal and updating of the world-Church.

Notes

1. John W. O'Malley, *What Happened at Vatican II*, Cambridge, Mass., 2008, pp. 9, 37.
2. Patrick A. Kalilombe, 'The Effect of the Council on World Catholicism: Africa', in Adrian Hastings (ed.), *Modern Catholicism: Vatican II and After*, London, 1991, pp. 310–11.

3. Norman P. Tanner, *The Councils of the Church: A Short History*, New York, 2001, p. 111.
4. Tanner, *The Councils of the Church*, op. cit., p. 112.
5. Kalilombe, 'The Effect of the Council on World Catholicism', *op. cit.*, p. 311.
6. Curt Cadorette, *Catholicism in Social and Historical Contexts: An Introduction*, Maryknoll, New York, 2009, p. 183.
7. For example, the 'moratorium' debate advocated the suspension of foreign financial resources and missionary personnel to allow churches in Africa room to generate their resources locally. See Cedric Mayson, *Why Africa Matters*, Maryknoll, New York, 2010, pp. 134–5.
8. Laurenti Magesa, *Anatomy of Inculturation: Transforming the Church in Africa*, Maryknoll, New York, 2004, p. 130.
9. Pew Forum on Religion and Public Life, *Global Christianity: A Report on the Size and Distribution of the World's Christian Population* (December 2011), http://www.pewforum.org/uploadedFiles/Topics/Religious_Affiliation/Christian/Christianity-fullreport-web.pdf. Accessed on 28 December 2011.
10. See Walbert Bühlmann, *The Coming of the Third Church*, Slough, 1976; Philip Jenkins, *The Next Christendom: The Coming of Global Christianity*, Oxford, 2002.
11. See John L. Allen, *The Future Church: How Ten Trends are Revolutionizing the Catholic Church*, New York, 2009, pp. 13–53.
12. See Pope Benedict XVI, *Africae Munus* (Post-synodal Apostolic Exhortation), 19 November 2011; Agbonkhianmeghe E. Orobator, 'Introduction: the Synod as Ecclesial Conversation', in Agbonkhianmeghe E. Orobator (ed.), *Reconciliation, Justice, and Peace: the Second African Synod*, Maryknoll, New York, 2011, pp. 1–3.
13. Robert G. Donders, *Non-Bourgeois Theology: An African Experience of Jesus*, Maryknoll, New York, 1985, p. 189.
14. Elochukwu E. Uzukwu, *A Listening Church: Autonomy and Communion in African Churches*, Maryknoll, New York, 1996, p. 59.
15. [Tr.: 'a theology of African colour] T. Tshibangu, *La théologie africaine*, Kinshasa, DRC, n. d., p. 56; A. Ngindu Mushete, *Les thèmes majeurs de la théologie africaine*, Paris, 1989, pp. 42–7.
16. John Parratt, *Reinventing Christianity: African Theology Today*, Grand Rapids, MI, 1995, p. 11.
17. See a more extensive account in Parratt, *Reinventing Christianity*, pp. 1–24.
18. Laurenti Magesa, 'On Speaking Terms: African Religion and Christianity in Dialogue', in Orobator, *Reconciliation, Justice, and Peace*, op. cit., p. 26.
19. Robert J. Schreiter, *Constructing Local Theologies*, Maryknoll, New York, 1985, p. 29.
20. Laurenti Magesa, 'The Council of Trent and the African Experience', in James F. Keenan (ed.), *Catholic Theological Ethics Past, Present, and Future*, Maryknoll, New York, 2011, p. 53.
21. Magesa, *Anatomy of Inculturation*, op. cit., p. 42; Jean-Marc Ela, *My Faith as an African*, Maryknoll, New York & London, 1988, pp. 47–50 (Eng. trans. of *Ma foi d'Africain* (1985).
22. Aylward Shorter, *Toward a Theology of Inculturation*, Maryknoll, New York, 1988, pp. 191–5.
23. Examples include eucharistic liturgies, initiation rites, consecration rituals, liturgical music, and worship gestures in West, Central, and East Africa. See Elochukwu E. Uzukwu, *Worship as Body Language: Introduction to Christian Worship: An Orientation*, Collegeville, MN, 1997, pp. 270–317; *A Listening Church*, op. cit., p. 62.

24. Uzukwu, *Worship as Body Language*, pp. 30–4.
25. Magesa, *Anatomy of Inculturation, op. cit.,* p. 234.
26. 'Pope John's Opening Speech to the Council', on 11 October 1962, in W. M. Abbot (ed.), *The Documents of Vatican II*, London & Dublin, 1966, p. 712.
27. Karl Rahner, 'Basic Theological Interpretation of the Second Vatican Council', in *Concern for the Church: Theological Investigations XX*, London & New York, 1981, p. 80.
28. Kalilombe, 'The Effect of the Council on World Catholicism', *op. cit.*, p. 310.
29. Giuseppe Alberigo & Joseph A. Komonchak (eds), *History of Vatican II,* vol. I, English ed., Maryknoll, New York & Leuven, 1995, p. 390.
30. Alberigo & Komonchak, *History of Vatican II,* vol. I, *op. cit.*, p. 311.

North American 'Impulses' following Vatican II

MARY E. HINES

I Introduction

Asked to reflect on early impulses or directions from the years immediately following the Second Vatican Council in Canada and the United States, I have chosen one major event in each country that captures the enthusiasm right after the Council and has had a lasting impact. They are the Congress on the Theology of the Renewal of the Church held in Toronto in 1967 and the Call to Action Conference held in Detroit in 1976, almost ten years later. These two early events frame the period of early response to the Council and are symbolic of the directions, and eventually of the conflicts, that have come to characterize the post-Vatican II Church in North America.

The earlier event was convened by the Canadian Catholic bishops as the Catholic contribution to the celebration of the Centenary of Canada – 1867–1967 – held at the University of St Michael's College in Toronto in 1967, only two years after the close of the Council. Its proceedings were published in two volumes, one on religious thought and one on religious structure.[1] Inspired by Vatican II's call for renewal, the Congress took up many of its themes, and brought together many of the theological architects of conciliar thought from Europe and North America.[2] The Call to Action Conference, too, interestingly enough, was called by the US bishops (NCCB/USCC)[3] as part of the American Bicentennial Celebration. Perhaps both the Canadian and US bishops' decisions to be involved in nationwide civic celebrations were themselves significant responses to the message of *Gaudium et spes* that the Church had moved out of its world withdrawal period to a new era of engagement with the world. It is also noteworthy that both events were convened 'from above', by the Church's hierarchy, as was the Council itself. In more recent church experience, the relationship between governance 'from above' and calls for reform 'from below' that include the experience and concerns of the laity, has grown more contentious.

II Congress on the theology of the renewal of the Church

The Canadian congress was a largely intellectual response to the Council that reflected many themes from the contemporary North American cultural context. Its participants included Eastern Orthodox, Protestant and Jewish theologians. Speaking to the gathered theologians in his introductory address, Cardinal Léger, following *Gaudium et spes* 62, said, 'to fulfil this task [theological renewal] properly, the magisterium needs you and you need freedom. Your freedom is not only of importance, but is essential for your work. The fidelity of the theologian to the magisterium must not be interpreted as a passive obedience which excludes all initiative'.[4] A new freedom for responsible theological inquiry was an early and optimistic expectation of theologians in Canada and the United States. The nature and extent of this freedom has become an increasingly neuralgic issue in the ensuing post-conciliar era.

The papers from Volume 1 reveal an ongoing concern about secularism, modern atheism, death-of-God theologies and existentialism, concerns very alive in the European and North American climate of the 1960s.[5] Although Karl Rahner famously referred to the Council as the coming to be of the third great stage of Christianity,[6] a world Church that would grow out of and embody the diverse cultures that form the Church, these papers indicate that theology immediately following the Council was still dominated by western theologians and concerns, as was the Council itself.

Volume 2, however, on the renewal of Church structures, introduces topics that would dominate intra-church discussions over the next half-century. Cardinal Suenens in his introduction heralded co-responsibility as the 'dominating idea of the Council' and reflected on its pastoral consequences.[7] Greater involvement of the laity and the specific roles of theologians and scholars in 'forming the judgment of the Church'[8] were discussed and debated in the panels that followed the papers. Theological education for the laity and their consultation on matters of human sexuality were specific topics, as were ecumenism and the relationship of

Church and world. The roles of women in the Church were not addressed specifically in the addresses. There were a few women contributors, but women appeared in the papers only in the context of family, sexuality and religious life. Inevitably, however, the overarching theme of co-responsibility soon led to demands for women to be included explicitly in the newly-awakened consciousness of lay persons that 'We are the Church!' This became an early slogan for the anticipated post-Vatican II renewal in North America.

It is no accident that shortly after the intellectual ferment created by this conference the University of St Michael's College, site of the Congress, became a leader in educating large numbers of the earliest generation of lay Catholic theologians, including women. St Michael's was uniquely positioned to play this role because of developments in its theological degree programs that had begun in the years preceding the Council.[9] St Michael's had awarded the STB degree since 1955, primarily as an ordination requirement for Basilian seminarians. In 1958, on the eve of the Council, the Faculty of Theology at St Michael's was created, and in 1962 and 1964 the MA and PhD programmes were launched. These programmes were designed for lay persons and from the beginning as many women as men were admitted. Shortly thereafter, in 1965, the St Michael's graduate programme in theology became part of an ecumenical graduate school of theology that would evolve into the Toronto School of Theology, a working ecumenical consortium that put into practice the ecumenical intentions of the Council.

Vatican II and the Toronto congress were catalysts for the excitement about theological study that drew so many lay men and women to become theologians in the years following the Council. The changing nature of the theological enterprise in North America is captured by the demographic change in the membership of the Catholic Theological Society of America, almost entirely clerical in membership through the 1960s. Lay men and women theologians in large numbers are now integral to the CTSA both as members and as officers.

III Call to action

Many of these same themes characterized early enthusiasms in the United States, but with differences in emphasis and style. Call to Action took place almost ten years after the Toronto Congress and centred on two themes that captured the attention of many in the US Church: first, the Council's call to dialogue with the world; and, second, the emphasis on collegiality, which came to be broadly interpreted as a desire to include all levels of the Church in participatory decision-making, or co-responsibility, as Cardinal Suenens termed it. The immediate impetus for the NCCB's choice of theme was the 1971 Synod document, *Justice in the World*, which developed the Council's call to 'read the signs of the times'. Justice became the overall theme of the conference. The insistence of *Gaudium et spes* that, '[t]he joys and the hopes, the griefs and the anxieties of the men [sic] of this age, especially those who are poor or in any way afflicted, these too are the joys and hopes, the griefs and anxieties of the followers of Christ. Indeed, nothing genuinely human fails to raise an echo in their hearts' (LG 1)[10] inspired the choice of the major topics which Call to Action proposed for consideration. The human being is *imago Dei* and deserves human dignity, human rights, social and economic justice. Among the issues tackled were racism, poverty, violence and war. The goal of the conference was to develop an action plan to address these issues. Cardinal Dearden, Detroit's archbishop and chairman of the NCCB Ad Hoc Committee for the Bicentennial, in his opening address also saw the conference as a way to spread more widely the Council's message of social justice to Catholics not yet aware of the Council's teaching.[11] The Vatican Council's embrace of collegiality (LG 22) found particular resonance in the USA and created an early expectation of a more participatory style of church governance at every level of church life. The Call to Action process followed a format that involved widespread consultations and hearings on conference topics in the two years prior to the conference. It brought together US democratic procedures with the conciliar encouragement of dialogue and involvement of the laity. Cardinal Dearden commented: 'Never before has there been an attempt to bring together in this way representatives of the whole ecclesial community of the United States: bishops, priests, religious, and laity.'[12] Things looked promising for cooperation and dialogue between hierarchy and laity in pursuit of the Church's mission.

Discussion and debate about the Church's response to pressing social-justice issues led inevitably to questions about justice within the Church. The 1971 Synod had made the statement, 'While the Church is bound to give witness to justice, she recognizes that anyone who ventures to speak to people about justice must first be just in their eyes. Hence we must undertake an examination of the modes of acting and of the possessions and life style found within the Church herself.'[13] The delegates to Call to Action took up this challenge. While agreeing that the Church should confront racism, sexism, militarism and economic injustice, they also raised questions about the actual involvement of every level of the Church in important inner-church decisions. The purely consultative nature of dialogic structures from parish councils to synods gave the laity no deliberative voice. Delegates called the Church to re-evaluate its positions on ecclesially sensitive issues such as priestly celibacy, birth control, homosexuality and a male-only clergy.

As a result many bishops gradually distanced themselves from this collaborative effort. Call to Action reinvented itself as a primarily lay organization that is now often viewed by the bishops as antagonistic – just the opposite of what they had intended when they themselves initiated the Call to Action process. Dialogue and cooperation continued to some extent through the 1980s with the widely consultative processes that the US bishops employed to compose their pastoral letters on peace and the economy.

No such positive dialogue occurred on the inner-church issues or issues of personal morality, and the chasm between bishops and laity has been widened over the handling of the sexual-abuse scandal in the US. The hoped-for cooperative relationship among hierarchy and laity, including theologians, has been further compromised by the disciplining of theologians, most often without dialogue.[14] The more dialogical and inclusive Church envisioned by the Toronto Congress, the early period of Call to Action and the pastoral letters seems an ever more elusive goal.

IV Conclusion

I have highlighted through the lens of the Toronto Congress and the 1976 Call to Action Conference some early hopes and expectations following the Council in North America. The relationship of Church and world, exercise of authority in the Church, freedom of theological inquiry, expanded roles for the laity, the emergence of a new and enthusiastic cadre of lay theologians, and ecumenism as the appropriate context in which to pursue theological reflection on the Church, emerged as motifs of the North American theological scene in the immediate years following the Council.

In more recent years, it has become clear that church-world dialogue can be conflictual as Church and world engage with the difficult social and ethical issues of the time. Lay persons have come to expect greater voice both in the Church's relation to society and within the Church. The priest shortage and the sexual-abuse scandal have also contributed to lay persons' sense of ownership and desire to contribute their experience to church leadership. Within the North American context the issue of married men and women's ordained leadership has become symbolic of the desire for a more inclusive Church at all levels.

Fifty years later, the Church is markedly different from its pre-Vatican II reality. The question remains whether it will continue along the path opened up by Pope John XXIII and the Council, and envisioned by early responses, or retreat to a pre-conciliar ecclesial world view. I hope that the 'dangerous memory' of the enthusiasm and energy for a more inclusive and dialogical Church that characterized early reception of the Council can reinvigorate that desire for reform and renewal, especially among younger Catholics in North America, who often have not been introduced to the dramatic event that was the Second Vatican Council, and for whom the Church is an increasingly irrelevant reality.

Notes

1. L. K. Shook, CSB (ed.), *Theology of Renewal*, vol. 1, *Renewal of Religious Thought;* vol. 2, *Renewal of Religious Structures*, New York, 1968. Hereafter: *TR* 1, *TR* 2.
2. The CBC [Canadian Broadcasting Corporation] broadcast four half-hour programmes in 1968 called *Theologo '67* which also documented the Congress's proceedings. The programmes focused on poverty, war, contraception, Church and world, church unity, and conscience.
3. Now the USCCB.
4. P.-É. Léger, 'Theology of the Renewal of the Church', in *TR* 1, p. 21.
5. See, for example, the essays by Schillebeeckx (pp. 83–104), Rahner (pp. 167–92); Mascall (pp. 193–207); Gibson (pp. 313–28) and Fabro (pp. 329–55) in *TR* 1.
6. K. Rahner, 'Basic Theological Interpretation of the Second Vatican Council', *Theological Investigations XX: Concern for the Church*, New York, 1981, pp. 77–83.
7. L-J. Suenens, 'Co-responsibility: Dominating Idea of the Council and its Pastoral Consequences', in *TR* 2, pp. 7–18.
8. R. A. F. Mackenzie, SJ, 'The Function of Scholars in Reforming the Judgment of the Church', in *TR* 2, pp. 118–32.
9. I rely for this information on an unpublished paper on the history of theology at St Michael's College by W. H. Irwin, CSB, former Dean of the Faculty of Theology.
10. Quotations from Vatican II are from W. M. Abbott (ed.), *The Documents of Vatican II*, New York, 1966.
11. Documents and early analyses of the Call to Action may be found at http://cta-

usa.org/whobishconference. *Origins* (vols 6–9) is also a source of documentation and early analysis.
12. J. F. Dearden, 'Opening Address', http://www.justpeace.org/NCCB101976.htm.
13. *Justice in the World*, USCC Publications Office, Washington DC, 1972, ch. 3.
14. For a balanced and more extended analysis of the hopes for dialogue initiated by the Call to Action Conference, see Bradford Hinze, *Practices of Dialogue in the Roman Catholic Church*, New York, 2006, pp. 64–89.

Vatican II Fifty Years Later in Latin America and the Caribbean

JOSÉ OSCAR BEOZZO

The years of the Council brought a breath of fresh air to the whole of the Church on the Latin American continent, while at the same time political coups inspired by the confrontations of the Cold War established military dictatorships in most of our countries for over 30 years. Sectors of the Church committed to the elimination of poverty, inequalities and injustices and the defence of human rights clashed with the dictatorships and suffered heavy repression, including the arrest, torture and murder of their leaders.

The main impacts of Vatican II were the result of the rediscovery and deepening of collegiality between the churches of Latin America and the Caribbean and were collected, organized and reinterpreted in the light of the urgent need for change in the economic, political, social and religious situation of the continent by the General Conferences of the Latin American bishops.

At the Second General Conference, in Medellín, Colombia, in 1968, the main emphasis was on the situation of poverty and severe injustice affecting the majority of the population, and the need for a Church of service, of one community wholly committed to the poor and their liberation.

The Third Conference, in Puebla, Mexico, in 1979, declared that the suffering face of Christ must be sought in the sufferings, past and present, of indigenous people, African slaves, rural people and workers, the unemployed and excluded, among young people and children, women and old people, and that all areas of human life, economic, social, political and cultural, needed to be permeated by faith and evangelization, with a preferential option for young people and the poor, who were seen as the subjects of a liberating evangelization. The following years brought painful experiences. Church communities, often the poorest and most harassed by the repression of the military dictatorships, also suffered repression from the Church, notably their catechists, pastoral workers, religious, theologians and even bishops and bishops' conferences that supported them. The Vatican Instruction *On Some Aspects of the Theology of Liberation* (6 August 1984) cast a shadow over the journey of these churches and the biblical, theological and pastoral reflection that accompanied it. The heaviest criticisms were directed at the supposed immanentist and one-sided character of Christians' action for liberation and the uncritical use of analytical tools inspired by various strands of Marxist thought. Along with the criticism came punishment for well-known theologians. The strong reaction of the Brazilian bishops' conference (CNBB) led to the publication of a second Instruction that recognized the positive aspects of this church journey and the theology of liberation: *Instruction on Christian Freedom and Liberation* (23 March 1986). After a meeting with the leadership of the CNBB, the cardinals, and the presidents of its seventeen regions in March 1986, John Paul II lifted the silence imposed on the theologian Leonardo Boff and sent a personal letter to the Brazilian bishops in which he declared: 'You and we are convinced that the theology of liberation is not only opportune, but useful and necessary.' He went on to give the CNBB the task of monitoring the theology of liberation in Brazil and the rest of the continent: 'I think that in this field the Brazilian Church can play a role both important and delicate, that of creating the space and conditions for the development, in complete harmony with the fruitful teaching contained in the two Instructions mentioned [*Libertatis nuntius* and *Libertatis conscientia*], of a theological reflection that adheres fully to the constant teaching of the Church on social issues and is at the same time capable of inspiring effective action for social justice and equity, the safeguarding of human rights and the building of a human society based on harmony, truth and charity. In this way, it would be possible to break the supposed inevitability of the systems – both unable to guarantee the liberation brought by Jesus Christ – of unrestrained capitalism and collectivism or state capitalism (cf *Libertatis conscientia* 10, 13). Fulfilling this role would be a service that the Brazilian Church could perform for its own country and the quasi-continent of Latin America, and indeed for many other regions of the world in which the same challenges appear with similar force. To fulfil this role there is no alternative to the wise and courageous action of pastors, that is, yourselves. May God help you to maintain a constant watch to ensure that this correct and necessary theology of liberation develops in Brazil and Latin America, homogeneously and not heterogeneously with the theology of all the ages, in complete fidelity to the teaching of the Church and careful to foster a preferential love for the poor that is not excluding or exclusive'.[1]

The Fourth Conference, in Santo Domingo, in the Caribbean, in 1992, emphasized the leadership of lay men and women, and especially of young people, for a 'new and culturally sensitive evangelization among indigenous peoples, African-Americans, people of mixed race and in modern urban culture and the mass media, imbued with work for all-round human advancement, based on a renewed, gospel-based option for the poor, in the service of Life and the Family'.[2]

The Fifth Conference, in Aparecida, Brazil, in 2007, in the new context of a globalization producing exclusion and a serious environmental crisis, reaffirmed the broad lines of the journey of the People of God in Latin America and the Caribbean, marked by the blood of so many martyrs, and proposed a revival of Church base communities and the commitment to liberation. It called on all the baptized to become disciples and missionaries of Christ, in a great endeavour of evangelization and work for integral human advancement.

In church terms, these conferences represent a fuller and more deliberative exercise of episcopal collegiality, with a magisterium of their own, in contrast to the diminished and merely consultative role of the Synod of Bishops.

The most significant and creative part of the Council's legacy was the so-called 'popular reading of the Bible', a vast communal appropriation of the Word of God that provided sustenance for the church base communities and social ministries through these years and in which the laity, and especially women, were often the leaders.

On a continent where missionary work came hand in glove with political conquest and economic exploitation, and the imposition of the language, culture and religion of the conquerors, the Council's proposal of a Church structured as the people of God and of a liturgy respectful of local customs and cultures led to a process of liberating cultural adaptation that often produced conflict. From Tarahumara in the north of Mexico to the Chiapas highlands in the south, in Guatemala, Ecuador, Bolivia and Peru, in the wake of the debates provoked by the 500th anniversary of the arrival of Europeans (1492–1992), countless indigenous peoples began to insist on their own identity and opened up a fruitful dialogue between the Gospel and their ancestral cultures. They reclaimed their spiritual roots, began to value their rites and customs and began to develop an indigenous theology and build a Church with indigenous features. Among African-Americans there was a similar movement to eliminate discrimination and racism in the churches as well as in wider society, to rediscover and transcend a history marked by almost four centuries of slaver States. They began to base liturgical celebrations on their roots, resistance and struggles and to construct a black theology of liberation.

What are the new challenges that our societies and Church are likely to face in the future? Some are old, but still persist, such as the elimination of extreme poverty and extreme social inequality, of the lack of land for rural people to work or for decent housing in cities, lack of work for young people, lack of health care, education and security for all. Among the new challenges, the following stand out:

a) The worsening of the environmental crisis caused by the increasingly rapid destruction of the Amazon rainforest and other biospheres on the continent, the desertification of entire regions, an increasing lack of fresh water, the pollution of rivers, lakes and oceans, and of the air and land in big cities, the worrying contamination of foods by the indiscriminate use of agricultural chemicals, or hormones and antibiotics in the breeding of fish and poultry, or preservatives and colourings in processed foods. The Church has helped to raise awareness of this crisis and of the fact that our future, and especially the future of the coming generations, depends on the care we have for nature, and that there is a close relationship between our lives and the life of the planet, and that attacks on it are attacks on human life. An increasing number of people, like Sister Dorothy Stang, lose their lives because of their opposition to the predatory exploitation of natural resources. They are the new martyrs in the same battle for life: defending life now means defending environmental rights, as well as the political, social and personal rights of the poorest. This is leading to a review in biblical studies, theology and catechetics, giving us a more accurate exegesis in which God's order to humans to subdue the earth in no way authorizes us to destroy it, but rather implies increased responsibility to preserve it and restore it.

b) Religious pluralism: Latin America and the Caribbean have always had a variety of religious traditions: in the over two thousand original peoples that existed here before the arrival of the Europeans, in the millions of slaves brought from different regions and cultures of Africa, and in the mass European and Asian immigration from the second half of the nineteenth century onwards. This did not prevent Latin America from becoming a mainly Catholic continent, at least nominally. The new phenomenon today is the proliferation of religious experiences of all sorts, and the re-emergence of indigenous and African American religions, together with the large number of people who change religion.

There are two apparently contradictory features in this area: on the one hand, a veritable explosion of religion, particularly visible in the multiplication of Pentecostal and neo-Pentecostal churches, and, on the other, a disaffection from the more institutionalized religious forms of the traditional churches. At the extreme, people say they have 'no religion', and this is the segment that has grown most rapidly over the last thirty years among the population in general, but especially in urban centres. There is another new factor in these forms of unbelief: they are also widespread among the traditionally religious poorer sectors. In this respect, they differ from the classical agnosticism of intellectuals as a result of conflicts between religion and science. They also differ from the tendency of 'loss of faith' in the working class as a result of the Church's accommodation with the bourgeois sectors of society, and its political alliance with conservative parties against the Socialist, Anarchist, Communist and other left-wing parties aligned with the interests of the workers in the conflicts between capital and labour. The phenomenon is particularly visible in the poor districts on the outskirts of great conurbations, in the dormitory towns beside industrial areas, and in the shanty-towns and slums of the inner cities.

c) The Pentecostalization of Christianity: If we can distinguish three main expressions of Christianity, that of the ancient East, that of the Latin West and that of the Protestant Reformation, it is now necessary to add a fourth, that of Pentecostalism, espoused by a quarter of today's two billion Christians. Alongside the Pentecostal churches and movements, the charismatic movement is showing notable strength, both within the Protestant churches, such as the Anglicans, the Lutherans, the Methodists and the Presbyterians, and within the Catholic Church. In this sense, in parallel with the growth of Pentecostalism in Latin America and the Caribbean, there is also a Pentecostalization of large sectors of Catholicism, mainly among the middle and upper classes.

d) The religious message has become a media event: The churches that have shown the most dramatic growth are those for which large-scale use of the media was most central to their strategy, first radio and television and now the internet. The phenomenon of the 'electronic churches' of the United States is being replicated in Latin America and the Caribbean, with the spread of a 'gospel' culture that pervades various churches indiscriminately. Singing pastors and priests and big religious music festivals are becoming the most frequent manifestations of this strand of religion, which combines emotion and subjectivity with huge collective 'happenings', but has little doctrinal basis and minimal social or political involvement arising from its faith.

e) The massification and anonymity of urban society: In the last 50 years, the whole continent has experienced extremely high rates of urbanization, fed by massive migration from country to city, from the small and medium urban centres to the great metropolitan conurbations. Mega-cities such as Mexico City or São Paulo, metropolitan centres like Santiago in Chile, Bogotá in Colombia, Lima in Peru, Rio de Janeiro in Brazil and Buenos Aires in Argentina, have transformed the human and social landscape of the continent. For a Catholicism that flourished in rural settings and small towns, it has become a huge challenge to respond to the new questions and demands of urban society and find ways of creative and prophetic engagement with the mega-cities, in a context of open religious competition and alternative life-styles, lacking any dimension of transcendence.

We need to review and reinvent the Council to meet the challenges of today.

Translated by Francis McDonagh

Notes

1. John Paul II, *Mensagem do Santo Padre ao Episcopado do Brasil, Vaticano, 9 de abril de 1986*, São Paulo, 1986, No. 5.
2. Santo Domingo document 302–3.

The Reception of Vatican II in a Multireligious Continent

FELIX WILFRED

I Asians–active agents of their faith

One of the beautiful things about Vatican II was its great spirit of freedom in Christian life. Thanks to it, for the first time Asian Christians became active agents in the practice of their faith. There was a sense of freedom, unfettered by the past, to shape the way they worship, and understand and interpret Christian faith. It was this freedom that brought about renewal in the Christian communities, and facilitated the bridging of faith and culture and evolving of innovative theological perspectives. By and large, the mission history in Asia has been one in which the people of the continent were passive recipients of a message preached to them, objects to be spiritually acted upon. The greatest contribution of Vatican II to Asia has been to have made Asian Christians active agents. In other words, it contributed to the maturing of Asian Christians. What happened at the Asian Synod of 1998 could be viewed as the result of this maturation process set free by Vatican II. At the Synod, 'What was new is not what the Asian bishops said, but *that* they said and *how* and *where* they said. In front of the pope and the Roman Curia, with surprising boldness and candour, they humbly learn from but also have something to teach the Church of Rome as well as the universal Church, precisely from their experiences as churches not simply *in* but of Asia'.[1]

II The three dialogues

The Federation of Asian Bishops' Conferences (FABC) became the catalyst and clearing house for the major ideas and orientations of Vatican II.[2] It is this body which translated the dialogical impetus of Vatican II in Asia in three major directions most relevant to the situation of Asia: dialogue with *cultures*, with *religions* and with *the poor*.³ Most stimulating reinterpretation of Christian faith took place in Asia not by the reading of Christian dogmas through Asian conceptual categories, as through the concrete dialogical praxis in these three major areas. The new conception of culture (far from the evolutionary one) to be found throughout the documents of the Council, and the orientations of *Nostra aetate* provided the seminal thoughts to develop dialogue with cultures and religions. As is well-known, though there was no focused treatment on the 'Church of the Poor' (Pope John XXIII), the Council did speak of the poor. In fact, Vatican II is only the second council in the history of the Church which spoke of the poor, the first being the Council of Jerusalem, which gave the injunction to 'remember the poor'.⁴ The spirit of the Council and the stimulus it gave led the Asian churches to engage themselves in dialogue with the poor, and rightly so. For Asia is still the home for the greatest number of the poor in the world. The numerous initiatives of the Federation of Asian Bishops' Conferences have again and again with insistence come back on the realities and experiences of the poor of the continent. This is true also of some of the local churches. As Bishop Bacani noted with reference to the situation in his country, 'The Church of the Poor is the Church in the Philippines' way of receiving and inculturating one of the most potent but undeveloped seeds which Vatican II sowed in the Lord's orchard. There was enough in Vatican II to inspire Medellín and Puebla to a new way of evangelization. There was enough in Vatican II to inspire the church in the Philippines also towards a new way of being Church'.⁵

III   Unfazed Asians sing their own tunes

The vitality behind Vatican II is often characterized as *ressourcement*.⁶ Asian Christians found the return to the *pluralism* of earliest Christian tradition consonant with the Asian cultural ethos. Be it in the field of Christian worship, theological developments, interpretation of Scriptures or shaping of the life of the local communities, Asian Christians worked out, thanks to the Council, ways to be themselves, without having to conform to any single pattern. The centralizing type of universality seemed to wane, giving place to the pluralism of Pentecost (Acts 2.1–12).

It was the deep imbibing of Vatican II that prompted the Asian Churches to view with apprehension some of the Roman positions, which they felt were going contrary to the spirit of the Council. Whereas Rome has been loud on explicit preaching of the Gospel, baptism and conversion, Asian bishops and the Asian Christians have been quietly insisting that the kind of mission most effective in the continent is that of silent witnessing. While Roman documents laid stress on preaching Jesus Christ as the only Saviour, Asian Churches focused on following the path of historical Jesus in his commitment to the poor, in his spirit of dialogue and in his way of life reaching out to the other. This, they felt, was the way to gain a deeper understanding of the mystery of Jesus Christ. As the Japanese Bishops' Conference wrote in their response to the *Lineamenta* of the Asian synod, 'Jesus Christ is the Way, the Truth and the Life, but in Asia, before stressing that Jesus Christ is the Truth, we must search much more deeply into how he is the Way and the Life'.[7] Here, we find reflected the absorption of the pastoral nature of Vatican II. That the Asian Churches have consistently maintained all this is itself a great sign of the continued reception of Vatican II, unfazed by the trends of restoration and integrism. Suffused with the spirit of pluralism, diversity and dialogue, Asia is probably too elusive to allow itself to be framed within such trends, as many interventions of the bishops showed at the Asian Synod.

IV Carrying forward a legacy

Asian Churches not only have tried to implement Vatican II, but also in some crucial areas have carried forward the Council one step further. I should mention at least two important areas: one is *theology of religions*, and the other the *understanding of mission*. Though in Asia there have been fresh thinking and initiatives to relate to peoples of other faiths right from the nineteenth century,[8] it was with Vatican II that inter-religious dialogue became programmatic and got a new impetus. Asian theologians have drawn not only from *Nostra aetate* but also important insights from other documents such as *Gaudium et spes* and *Lumen gentium* to build a relevant theology of religions. If we read the conciliar texts LG 16, GS 22, AG 22, DH 3 and NA 1 synoptically, they will take us to a broad vision of God's salvific plan for the entire human family across all borders, and make us realize that the responses in human freedom to the offer of God's grace take place through many channels. FABC and Asian theologians have been inspired by these texts and found them a great support in their work.[9] The actual practice of dialogue has helped them take the conciliar teachings forward to a new level. A reading of conciliar teachings coupled with praxis of dialogue made Asian churches realize that the Spirit of God is actively operative in and through the religious experience, symbols and signs of neighbours of other faiths; that we need to consider their scriptures seriously and ask whether they are also not inspired; and that other religions could be channels of God's salvific grace. Asian theologians went on to discuss against this background the question of *communicatio in sacris* with people of other faiths.

The theology of religions inspired by the Council, if taken seriously, needs to be matched by a new theology of mission. There has been a mismatch between the two in the post-conciliar period. For their part, Asian Christians have worked out an approach to mission that is in keeping with the conciliar theology of religion and its larger implications. On the other hand, they were told by Roman central offices to follow a theology of mission that again and again history has proved is not workable in the context of Asia. For example, Asian theologians have resisted efforts to make dialogue a *means* of mission, as they believe that dialogue has an intrinsic value in itself, and its own scope and dynamism, and cannot be turned into a means. Asian theologians felt that the spirit of the Council was vindicated by the event of Assisi in October 1986, when Pope John Paul brought together leaders of many religious traditions to be united in prayer. A further consolidation of conciliar teaching was the statement in *Redemptoris missio* that 'the Spirit's presence and activity affect not only individuals but also society and history, peoples, cultures and religions'.[10] I see in this statement an instance of the influence of Asian theology of religion on the universal Church. At the same time, Asian theologians have critically questioned some of the post-conciliar documents which, unlike the Council, exhibit a negative attitude to other faiths and their spiritual practices.

V Dark clouds

Some of the recent developments in the Church have been a matter of preoccupation for Asian Christians. They are convinced that one of the great innovations of Vatican II was to listen and celebrate God's Word in their own tongues, mindful of the words of *Sacrosanctum concilium* (the liturgical document of Vatican II), which says: 'The Church has no desire, not even in liturgy, to impose a rigid monolithic structure. Rather, on the contrary, it cultivates and encourages the gifts and endowments of mind and heart possessed by various races and peoples'.[11]

Worship in Christian communities in local languages and through their symbols and signs brought faith closer to life. The numerous creative initiatives in India, Indonesia, Japan and many other parts of the continent bear witness to the seriousness with which Asian Christians have put the Council into practice. But then, today, Asian Christians are aghast at the efforts to ease restrictions on the use of the Tridentine mass, of which they are not able to make much sense, and which is certainly bound to alienate Christians from their culture and tradition. These efforts have to be read in conjunction with the attempts to dampen Asian practices of inculturation. The spirit of the Christian Pentecost is that every language is the language of God, of the Spirit. The 'pastoral initiative' of the Tridentine mass, apparently intended to avoid a rift in the Church, can be the source of new division and dissension in Christian communities. More recent Roman efforts to water down inter-religious dialogue and initiatives have been no less preoccupying. This has justifiably raised alarm among Asian Christians.

VI Conclusion

It seems to me that in modern times there has been no other document so relevant for mission in Asia as *Gaudium et spes*, even though it was not the document that dealt explicitly with mission. Why? Here is a document with which one could sensibly begin a serious discourse on mission in this continent. Its orientation vibrated with Asian concerns. For one thing, here we do not find the kind of *triumphalism* and *self-righteousness* which are the major obstacle to the witnessing of the Gospel; instead, we find a humble recognition that the Church is groping and struggling with the rest of humanity[12], and that it has its own weakness among its members.[13] The document opens up a large space for dialogue and for a *missio inter gentes*. Finally, what is significant for Asians is not only what Vatican II taught. Even more important is the approach and orientation it adapted to the mystery of God, the world and humanity. Here lies the key to the understanding of what the Council taught. To sustain this orientation, there is a need for constant renewal. It is not something to be achieved once and for all or periodically, but should be the permanent characteristic in genuine Christian life. Asians carry forward the legacy of the Council in a living manner by trying to renew Christian life and mission in a multi-religious and pluri-cultural continent. It is challenging, of course; but it makes Christian life exciting as well.

Notes

1. Peter C. Phan, 'Reception of Vatican II in Asia: Historical and Theological Analysis', in *FABC Papers*, 117, Hong Kong, 2006.
2. At the institutional level, there have been assemblies of local Churches which helped to deepen the teachings of the Council and its orientation in the life and practice of Christians. By way of example, I may refer here to the *All India Seminar: Church in India Today* held in Bangalore, India, in 1969, with the participation of a large number of bishops, priests, religious and laity. Similarly, *The Second Plenary Council of Philippines* in 1991 could be viewed as an important milestone in the reception of Vatican II in that country.
3. These three dialogues announced by the First General Assembly of FABC (Taipei 1974) became programmatic for the subsequent developments in the thought of FABC and in its pastoral orientations.
4. Cf. Aloysius Pieris, *Give Vatican II a Chance*, Gonawala-Kelaniya, 2010, p. 44.
5. Theodoro C. Bacani, 'Church of the Poor: The Church in the Philippines' Reception of Vatican II', *East Asian Pastoral Review* 42 (2005) 1/2, p. 157.
6. Cf. Gabriel Flynn & Paul D. Murray, *Ressourcement. A Movement for Renewal in Twentieth-Century Catholic Theology*, Oxford, 2012.
7. Peter C. Phan (ed.), *The Asian Synod. Texts and Commentaries,* New York, 2002, p. 30.
8. Since about 100 years before Vatican II, there have been numerous initiatives (intellectual as well as practical) for dialogue with peoples of other faiths, especially in India. I may refer here to the original views and practices of the Indian thinker Brahmabandhab Upadhyaya (1861–1907) on Hindu–Christian relations; the work of J. N. Farquhar, *The Crown of Hinduism* (1915), where he presented the theory of Christianity as the fulfilment of other religions; the ashram movement which adopted the Hindu world-view and way of life to interpret Christianity.
9. Cf. FABC Plenary Assembly in Taipei (1974) Final Statement. See also: 'Theses on Interreligious Dialogue' by the Theological Advisory Committee of FABC. For the text, see: Felix Wilfred & J. Gnanapragasam (eds), *Being Church in Asia*, Manila, 1994.
10. Cf. *Redemptoris missio* 28–9.
11. SC 37.
12. Cf. Felix Wilfred, 'Asian Christianity and Modernity: Forty Years after Vatican II', *East Asian Pastoral Review* 42 (2005), 1/2, pp. 191–206.
13. Cf. GS 43.

Vatican II: Inspiration and Encouragement for the Church in Europe

MARTIN MAIER SJ

It is extremely difficult, if not impossible, to talk of a global impetus of Vatican II for the Roman Catholic Church in Europe. This is due to the complex reality of Europe, which is not clearly enough defined, historically, geographically, politically or culturally. It is also due to the complex reality of the Council, which cannot be reduced to its texts but rather set in motion a movement of change and renewal in the Catholic Church, which is very far from complete. Finally, it is due to the limited space available, and the fact that, unlike, say, the episcopal assembly at Medellín in 1968, there has been no comparable continental assembly for transmission and implementation of the Council in Europe.

With these difficulties and restrictions in mind, following the main themes of universal Church, justice, collegiality and participation, ecumenism and disputed reception, I shall try to give at least a summary account of some of the ways in which Vatican II has inspired and encouraged the Church in Europe.

I   The end of European Christianity

It is somewhat paradoxical to say that the Second Vatican Council was a Council with a strongly European emphasis, which introduced the end of the profoundly European influence on the Church. Vatican II was largely an ecclesiastical event dominated by European bishops and theologians. The ecumenical and liturgical movement and the biblical movement, which prepared the way for the decisive progress of the Council, were essentially located in the European Church. Yet, if we accept Karl Rahner's basic theological interpretation of Vatican II as the 'Church's first official self-realization as a *universal Church*',[1] the Council definitely marked the end of a Catholicity under European influence and domination. Rahner compared this transition from a western-Eurocentric to a polycentric universal Church with the historical break that took place at the beginning of church history with the transition from Jewish to pagan Christianity. He referred cautiously to the 'beginning of a beginning' and with farsighted acumen suggested that the process of creating an authentically universal Church would need time. In fact, he thought it would probably take a full century.

In accordance with the Council's dual basic ecclesiological orientation, the Church's self-realization as a universal Church can be interpreted in both an inwardly and an outwardly directed perspective. Inwardly, Vatican II reasserted the old *communio* structure in the sense of a 'community of churches' in contradistinction to the ecclesial image of Vatican I, which was unilaterally jurisdictional and central. Accordingly, the dogmatic constitution *Lumen gentium* stresses the autonomy of local churches compared with Rome. They are not seen as mere subsidiaries of Rome, but are, and are called, churches in the full sense: 'The Church of Christ is really present in all legitimately organized local groups of the faithful which, insofar as they are united to their pastors, are also quite appropriately called churches in the New Testament' (LG 26). Similarly, the decree on the Church's missionary activity *Ad gentes divinitus* talks of the local or particular church as one that 'must represent the universal Church as perfectly as possible' (AG 20). Therefore the particular churches are granted the same theological status as the universal Church.

Outwardly, the self-realization of the Catholic Church as a universal Church in compliance with Vatican II is associated with its assumption of its universal responsibility in a global perspective. The pastoral constitution *Gaudium et spes* was concerned expressly with the question of a new and more equitable international order. At the time, the Cold War called for a special emphasis on securing peace. The question of social justice on a world scale was also a topic of contemporary concern. There is a reference in this context to the scandal of several nations where Christians are in the majority and possess an abundance of riches, 'while others lack the necessities of life and are tortured by hunger, disease, and all kinds of misery' (GS 88). Since the gulf between rich and poor nations has grown even deeper in recent decades, these words have not lost any particle of their relevance. As a universal Church principally concerned to defend the poor and excluded, the Church must work for an economic order and a treatment of the environment which look to the future and try to promote the optimum conditions for the life of all humankind.

II The Church in the service of justice and peace

The history of the Catholic Church in Europe in modern times up to the Second Vatican Council was characterized by a combative rejection of enlightenment and modernity. The 'leap forward' which Pope John XXIII called for in his opening address at Vatican II was principally concerned with a revision of the relationship between the Church and the modern world. With the Council the Church surrendered its defensive mentality and contributed its self-understanding in service to the world and humanity. This is expressed in more specifically theological terms in *Lumen gentium*: 'The Church in Christ is in the nature of sacrament—a sign and instrument, that is, of communion with God and of unity among all people' (LG 1).

This was tantamount to a Copernican turning-point. It was no longer its own interests and rights that were at the heart of the Church but the welfare of humans, of all humankind. For John XXIII, as he stated in his historic opening address at Vatican II: 'The Church should no longer concern itself with its own problems but serve all humanity in their search for justice, freedom and unity.'[2] He cited the social and political sphere as the responsibility of the Church. This message was all but echoed in the words of Pope Paul VI in his address the day before the Council closed: 'The Church has declared itself so to speak to be the servant of humankind, precisely when the celebration of the Council has made its magisterium and pastoral ministry more radiant and forceful: the idea of service has occupied a central position'.[3] The Church addressed all human beings, irrespective of their denomination or religious adherence. After long and strenuous resistance, it now adopted the idea of human rights.

III Collegiality and participation

An important impulse of Vatican II was the reinforcement of the collegial and synodal principle in the Church. Shortly before the end of the Council, Paul VI instituted episcopal synods, and the first full assembly was held in 1967. Of course bishops' conferences existed to some extent before the

Council, but Vatican II made them obligatory for the whole Church. The cooperation of bishops' conferences in different parts of the world was organized in continental councils. The Council of European Bishops' Conferences (CCEE) was set up in 1971 and now comprises thirty-three bishops' conferences. Pastoral and priests' councils were established at diocesan level.

The new participation of the laity in forms of church service accords with this tendency. The Council dismissed the model of a Church based on the notion of a pyramid with the pope, bishops and priests at the top, and laypeople subordinate and inferior to them. Instead, Vatican II promulgated the understanding of the Church as the people of God, with the primary emphasis on the common vocation of all the faithful, laity and clergy. The Council also expressly stated that laypeople should disclose to their pastor 'their needs and desires with that liberty and confidence which befits children of God and brothers and sisters in Christ. By reason of the knowledge, competence or pre-eminence which they have the laity are empowered (indeed sometimes obliged) to manifest their opinion on those things which pertain to the good of the Church' (LG 37). This lay expression of opinion has been institutionalized at diocesan level in the organs of diocesan pastoral councils and diocesan councils as well as asset management committees and diocesan synods.

IV The Church in the service of unity

Ecumenism is a special challenge for the churches of Europe, which is the continent of the Reformation and of the division of churches. John XXIII saw ecumenical unity as a central suasion for calling the Second Vatican Council. In the complex history of Europe, breaks between nations were often equivalent to separations between churches.[4] That denominational and religious differences still retain the potential to provoke violence was shown by the conflicts in former Yugoslavia. It is also urgent to reach an understanding between denominations and religions in view of the reinforcement of certain forms of nationalism in Europe, in which religious-denominational elements play a far from negligible part. If the churches wish to make a credible contribution to European unity, then they have to overcome their denominational divisions. The road to ecumenism is an essential condition for the realization of European unification.

Church unity is also strategically significant. The churches can compare their missions and visions with those of secular European institutions much more effectively if they do so jointly. The European ecumenical procedure introduced some 30 years ago is highly significant in this regard. It is supported by the Conference of European Churches (CEC), with a membership of 125 Anglican, Orthodox and Protestant Churches in almost all European countries, and by the Council of European Bishops' Conferences (CCEE). The European Ecumenical Assemblies in Basle (1989), Graz (1997) and Sibiu (2007) were decisive occasions for understanding between the Christian Churches of Europe.

The inception of the Ecumenical Charter (*Charta Oecumenica*)[5] in Strasbourg in 2001 was an important milestone in the development of this ecumenical process. It was signed by Metropolitan Jéremie Caligiorgis as President of the Conference of European Churches and by Cardinal Miloslav Vlk as President of the Council of European Bishops' Conferences. The Charter describes fundamental ecumenical tasks and associated guidelines and obligations. Although it has no status in canon law or as dogma or a document of the magisterium, the Charter is the most important document to date for a common project of the Christian Churches in Europe.

V The conflict about the reception and implementation of the Council

The Catholic Church in Europe today is still deeply affected by the conflict about the reception and implementation of the Council. To a certain extent, the conflict took forward into the process of post-conciliar reception and application the contention between a majority at the Council devoted to an opening up and renewal of the Church and a conservative minority bent on restoration. The forces that wish to dismantle many conciliar innovations and openings seem to have grown somewhat stronger. Actively traditionalist tendencies are also evident with regard to lay participation. For instance, the pastoral structural reforms in the German church would exclude laypeople from leading positions in the parish. The trend is towards a new clericalization of the Church at the very time when clergy numbers are constantly dwindling. Modern communication methods partly contributed to the intensification of the Roman centralism intent on rendering the Council null and void. The most worrying symptom of this tendency is the negotiations pursued since 2010 by the Vatican with the anti-conciliar Society of St Pius X. It seems reasonable to suspect that Vatican II is being used as a bargaining chip in these discussions.[6]

Basic church groups have been formed in various European countries to consolidate and extend the progress made by the Council. In Germany, for instance, an alliance of groups and institutions has called a conciliar assembly for October 2012 in Frankfurt am Main. The main task of this assembly will be to try to find answers in the spirit of the Council to urgent questions in the Church and the present-day world.[7]

Under the title *Eine Kirche, die Zukunft hat* (a Church with a future), Helmut Krätzl, a suffragan bishop in Vienna, has written twelve essays on 'seemingly insoluble problems in the Church'. His list includes who should be admitted to ordination in view of constantly growing number of parishes without priests; the status of bishops' conferences as constituting an intermediary body between the Pope, the Roman Curia and individual bishops; a new balance in the relationship between the universal Church and local churches; and a new definition of the role of women in the Church. With regard to the liturgy, Krätzl emphasizes the close connection between the renewal of the liturgy and that of the whole life of the Church. A return to the old liturgy could affect the entire renewal process in the Church.

Krätzl is convinced that the urgent problems in the Church cannot be solved by turning our backs on Vatican II. On the contrary, we have to work together in the Church to 'find ways that show us how to go forward in the spirit of the Council, and honestly admit that we were timorous and disinclined to risk far too few of the innovations which the Fathers of the Council had inspired and encouraged us to adopt'.[8]

Translated by J. G. Cumming

Notes

1. Karl Rahner, 'Theologische Grundinterpretation des II. Vatikanischen Konzils', in *id.*, *Schriften zur Theologie* XIV, Zürich, Einsiedeln & Cologne, 1980, p. 288.
2. Ludwig Kaufmann & Nikolaus Klein, *Johannes XXIII. Prophetie im Vermächtnis*, 2nd ed., Brig, 1990, p. 24.
3. Paul VI, 'Ansprache in der Öffentlichen Sitzung des Zweiten Vatikanischen Konzils (7. Dezember 1965)', in *Herders Theologischer Kommentar zum Zweiten Vatikanischen Konzil*, Peter Hünermann & Bernd Jochen Hilberath (eds), vol. 5: *Die Dokumente des Zweiten Vatikanischen Konzils: Theologische Zusammenschau und Perspektiven*, Freiburg im Breisgau, 2006, p. 570.
4. Cf. Jacques Le Goff, *L'Europe est-elle née au Moyen Age?*, Paris, 2003.

5. Cf. Nikolaus Klein, 'Strassburg – "Anfang eines Anfangs"?', *Orientierung* 65 (2001), pp. 121–4.
6. Cf. Andreas R. Batlogg, 'Das Konzil vor dem Ausverkauf?', *Stimmen der Zeit* 229 (2011), pp. 721–2.
7. See: www.pro-konzil.de.
8. Helmut Krätzl, *Eine Kirche, die Zukunft hat. 12 Essays zu scheinbar unlösbaren Kirchenproblemen*, Vienna, Graz & Klagenfurt, 2007, p. 9.

Comments on a Notification

ANDRES TORRES QUEIRUGA

On 30 April 2012, the Episcopal Commission for the Doctrine of Faith of the Spanish Bishops' Conference published a *Notification upon certain works of Professor Andrés Torres Queiruga*. This article is a short commentary on the contents of the Notification and a brief account of how it came about.

I The hermeneutics of the Notification

The document is clearly structured in three parts: Introduction, Analysis of the Points Discussed and Conclusion. It expressly says that it is not a condemnation and that it appreciates the work's good intentions, but it denounces 'deviations', listing them in seven questions which affect truths of the faith, and invites a response.

It begins by describing the author's *intention:* a 'concern to "rethink" traditional teaching, with the double purpose of making the proclamation of the faith comprehensible today' and presenting an image of God that is 'all love', remote from fear and threat. Then it adds its insistence on respecting creaturely autonomy.

It points out the *danger:* 'of reducing Christian faith to the categories of the dominant culture'. It goes on to pronounce *sentence:* the work has succumbed to the danger, because it does not admit the necessity for 'particular interventions' by God in the world, which leads to a 'rejection of the miracles, including the resurrection of Jesus Christ as a miracle that is susceptible to empirical proofs' *(sic)*.

The rest of the document consists of conclusions that could be drawn from the work *from this viewpoint.* I believe it is necessary to state that this interpretation violates fundamental standards of any proper hermeneutics.

1. It isolates particular questions from their global perspective and context. The Notification argues on the basis of three books: *Repensar la revelación. La revelación divina en la realización humana,* (Trotta, Madrid,

2008); *Dialogo de las Religiones y autocomprensión cristiana*, (Sal Terrae, Santander, 2005); *Repensar la resurrección. La diferencia cristiana en la continuidad de las religiones y de la cultura*, (Trotta, Madrid, ³2005). This selection betrays the absence of the many works where these matters are treated in detail, even leaving out some especially relevant works. In particular: *Constitución y evolución del Dogma*, Madrid, 1997 (doctoral thesis defended in the Gregorian), upon the historicity of theology; *La constitución moderna de la razón religiosa,* (Estella, 1992) and *Fin del cristianismo premoderno*, (Santander, 2000), about the cultural transformation of modernity; *Recuperar la creación*, (Santander, 1996), on creation for love; *Repensar el mal. De la ponerología a la teodicea* (Madrid,2010), on absolute divine goodness.

2. It begins by stating that the 'Episcopal Commission for the Doctrine of Faith has held an extensive thorough-going dialogue with the author'. Regardless of their subjective intention, I must state in conscience that this is not true. From 1998, the year in which the procedure began, until its conclusion in 2012, only *one* meeting lasting about two hours took place, on the eve of the document's approval in the Permanent Commission (of the Spanish Bishops' Conference). Before that, *no one* had *ever* officially sought or engaged in dialogue.

3. The structure of the interpretation shows a continual fluctuation between 'theology' and the 'faith' of the Church, together with a total lack of definition of the *ordinary* or *infallible* character of the term 'authentic' relating to the magisterium. The notes are a hotch-potch of conciliar declarations (unless otherwise decided by a competent authority, none of them infallible), together with papal documents, and documents of the Roman congregations and Spanish bishops. There is a plethora of quotations from the Catechism of the Catholic Church.

Judging a *theology* on these criteria constitutes a serious *metabasis eis allo genos* [genre shift], mixing without due distinction the 'catechetical and kerygmatic' with the 'theological and scientific', the *piscatorie* with the *aristotelice* [the 'fisherman-like' with the Aristotelian], as some Fathers put it. In current parlance, it confuses two different 'linguistic games' and two different 'intentionalities'. Such confusion goes against the essence of theological work, which even in recent official declarations, cannot be reduced to a mere gloss on the pastoral magisterium. Indeed, the document proceeds to identify a particular *theology* with the *faith* of the whole Church. Its general application would oblige it to condemn most theology:

even the Christology of Benedict XVI would not escape unscathed (that is why he says clearly 'anyone is free to contradict me').

It is painfully strange that upon these grounds an official pronouncement should place an interdict upon a theology, that like any human work is open for discussion, but which has always demonstrated scientific seriousness, an ecclesial spirit and readiness for dialogue. It is even stranger that it more or less directly accuses the work of denying fundamental truths of *faith*, listed at the end in seven alleged 'distortions', said to affect 'essential aspects of the doctrine of the Church' and to cause 'confusion among the People of God'.

Obviously, the *very fact* of an official declaration carries more weight than its actual *content*. I beg to state that pronouncing it *without any adequate basis* leads *objectively* to the spreading of serious 'calumnies'. A reading of some of the media and some of the blogs proclaiming themselves to be 'ultra-Catholic', which accuse me of 'heresy', because, supposedly, I deny the resurrection and other truths of the faith, shows that the danger is not imaginary. Some kinds of excessive zeal can also cause 'confusion among the People of God,' instead of educating them in the role of theology and gospel charity.

III Brief analysis of the points discussed

It would be useless to reply briefly to seven questions formulated without any personal dialogue and without that 'initial goodwill', which the pope himself requests for his work. If the work as a whole did not answer the questions, neither would a few short remarks. Furthermore, historical experience shows that the replies would never be accepted, as long as they did not correspond with what was expected, and the result would be to set me in a dark labyrinth from which there was no exit.

Neither is it possible here to analyse in detail the points criticized by the Notification: revelation, 'asymmetrical pluralism' in the dialogue between religions, the resurrection of Jesus Christ and problems of eschatology relating to the 'intervening time'. It is preferable to concentrate on a basic clarification and to indicate briefly the general direction of my replies.

My first impression, when I received the Notification (through the public media, not by personal communication) was the obvious *contrast* between what the actual quotations from the work say and the Notification's interpretations of them. This is so self-evident that nothing demonstrates it better than a reading of the document itself. It is worth quoting a text which comes at the beginning of the document and therefore decisively affects the central focus of my theology: *God-who-creates-for-love:* 'In this new paradigm the distinction does not seem to remain clear between creation and salvation. The author explains: "But if we take the Creator–creature relationship seriously, we must admit that God belongs to the 'nature' of this relationship, not, of course, as if he belonged to the world, but as the transcendent foundation of its very *being*. God is not 'outside', because *as Creator* he is always sustaining the creature; and by creating for love, he is never passive or indifferent, but is a saving and enlightening presence *for ever and for each man and woman*".'

The careful nuances of the texts (the italics are in the original) should reassure any objective hermeneutics. But the interpretation (with its style of indirect insinuation that ends up being a direct accusation) is reductive and unkind: 'The author's theological explanation would be acceptable as long as it did not reduce grace and blessedness to a mere development of nature, as if Christian life simply consisted in making explicit what was already implicit'.

Note that it says *mere* development of *nature*. 'Mere' is the typical, essentially reductive word (carefully avoided in my work) that this Commission also attributed to me on other occasions, and 'nature' remains abstract and undefined. It is only necessary to give it precision and omit the 'mere' to appreciate the real meaning: genuine 'development of nature' *insofar* as it is understood, specified and accepted by us *as based on and indwelt by God* through his ceaseless 'saving and enlightening presence for ever and for each man and woman'. This is the true meaning, that not only inspires all my theology, but which emerges self-evidently from the text. If this had been taken into account, it would have clarified the remaining replies.

To begin with *revelation* and its application to the *dialogue between religions* with its category of 'asymmetrical pluralism' (completed by the categories of 'inter-religionation' and 'Jesusian theocentrism'), it is hermeneutically cruel to state that I deny the novelty of revelation and its unsurpassable culmination in Christ. These are widely and expressly defended in my work, at the same time as I cordially welcome and respect what God – who 'wants all to be saved' – has revealed to other religions.

Taking into account the sharp express distinction made in my book between the radical experience of faith – 'that Jesus did not remain destroyed by death, but he himself in person continues to be alive and present, although in a new mode of existence – and also taking into account my various attempts at *theological explanation,* my treatment of the mystery of the *resurrection* is clearly within the bounds of normal theological pluralism. Denying the possibility of *empirical* 'apparitions' (and that is all we are talking about) is a position taken by many theologians today. 'The apparitions do not represent objectively determinable events,' says Cardinal Kasper. Perhaps there is a certain novelty in my unambiguous assertion of this viewpoint's consistency, when I state that postulating such 'apparitions' represents a covert *relapse into empiricism.* To demand physical proofs for the Risen One, who is now raised to Glory, would be *epistemologically* as incorrect as demanding proofs for the existence of God. *Ontologically,* it would contradict his universal presence in space and history. And *theologically* 'it would be grotesque to arrive thus at the inescapable conclusion that those who first announced the faith did not believe, because seeing dispensed them from faith' (Kasper).

As for affirming resurrection *already in death* and the non-necessity *for faith* of either the 'empty tomb' or of the 'intervening time' in eschatology, this represents the considered position of many important theologians today. As for 'prayer for the dead' and, more radically, 'prayer of *petition',* I have explained myself at length in other places. It is open for discussion and I understand that it would make necessary a profound liturgical revision; but at least it could be conceded that it tries to do justice to God's absolute initiative and fully respects his free love, that is nevertheless totally and irrevocably given: 'I stand at the door and knock' (Rev. 3.20).

IV   A brief account of how the document came about

Although in its immediately personal expressions about my intention the document shows some respect, for which I am grateful, I do not think it is wrong to say I consider it to be unfounded in its content, lacking in church fellowship in its procedure, and strange in its circumstances. A few points about its gestation may prove enlightening.

As I said, the *examination of my writings* began in the year 1998, without my knowing anything about it until 2012 – *for 13 years*! There was a *first draft* of the document, which is substantially little different from the present document (the latter improved in tone). Its publication, planned for 2009, was held up by public reaction when (having discovered this privately purely by chance) I made this plan known and also that it had been formed without any previous dialogue.

There was an *intermediate episode* in the year 2006 with the 'Pastoral Instruction of the Spanish Bishops' Conference', *Theology and Secularization in Spain.* Without naming me but with obvious quotations (and repeating the fateful 'mere'), a principal target of its criticism was my theology of revelation. I replied then with an explanatory article, which the current document quotes in its Galician version: 'Revelación como "caer na conta": razón teológica e maxisterio pastoral' in *Encrucillada* 149 (2006), pp. 357–73 (also published in Spanish: García Norro, J. J. (ed.), *Ser querido y querer,* Salamanca, 2007, pp. 73–192).

The *final stage* began on 10 January 2012, when my archbishop Julián Barrio summoned me. He was concerned, because he had been informed of the imminent publication of two documents, in Rome and in Madrid, criticizing my theology. He was doing his best to ensure that at least there would be a dialogue beforehand. I said I was not only ready but explicitly wanted this dialogue. Soon, it became clear that there was no document in Rome or any preparation for one.

On 30 January, I received a telephone call from Monsignor Adolfo Gonzalez Montes, the current President of the Commission. In a long and cordial conversation, we agreed to hold a meeting at which a bishop from the Commission would be present (Monsignor Enrique Benavent) and an external theologian (Professor Martín Gelabert, a Dominican). The date would be 27 February, as the Permanent Commission was meeting on the following day, and he wanted to present the document for its approbation. Despite this haste and the fact that he had told me that the decision had already been taken, so that it would only be possible to make a few slight modifications, I accepted in the hope that a revocation might be possible.

Fearing that everything would remain as a formal procedure (which is what happened), on the following day I wrote him a long private letter. In it, I reminded him that it was a question of conversing about matters of *faith,* not questions discussed in *theology,* I made two requests: an in-depth, contextualized study of the opinions in question and a commitment to seek only the truth. I concluded: 'I consider these two conditions to be so essential, that I beg you to make an opportunity at the beginning of the session for us to state expressly in the sight of the Lord–me first–that we are prepared to fulfil them'.

Knowing that it was difficult to fulfil them at such short notice, I suggested: 'If any of those attending the meeting, through lack of time or dedication to these topics, considers he is not prepared for this, I think the correct thing in his case would be to stand down from taking part in the dialogue. And in the last resort, it would always be an option to postpone the meeting until the conditions can be fulfilled in a satisfactory manner'.

The *meeting* took place on 27 February. It lasted about two hours and had a cordial conversational tone, with some theological clarifications, given by me and the checking of any conflict with any text of the *ordinary* magisterium. For his part, the invited theologian expressly recognized (as he later repeated in public) that nothing that was discussed went beyond legitimate theological pluralism. On the following day, the Permanent Commission approved the document (apparently leaving open the possibility of some modification).

Some time later, my archbishop sent me an *official letter*, in which, to my surprise, I was asked to reply to seven questions, clarifying what, according to my theology, 'is the faith of the Church and what is theological interpretation'. He gave as his reason that at the meeting 'we discovered that some of your theological proposals are incompatible with the faith of the Catholic Church'. Astonished at this statement, I replied officially that I found it 'literally incredible'.

I also made clear my disappointment because, although I had known we had been talking 'about *a decision that had already been taken*', I had agreed to it, thinking that 'if the matter was gone into thoroughly and with all the guarantees, it would clearly be seen how unsubstantiated were the suspicions about my theology *in matters of faith*'. I communicated my decision not to reply to the questions, because if reading the work itself 'had not explained my position clearly, then necessarily brief explanations without their full context would do so even less.' Furthermore, it would be a sort of endorsement of a whole procedure, which I consider to be *theologically* unfounded *and ecclesially* illegitimate.

Even so, a few days after the ICT (International Theological Commission) *Theology Today* had appeared, I made a *final request*. According to that document 'no one is in a better position to help Catholic theologians in their effort to offer the best possible service, in accordance with the true characteristics of their discipline, than other Catholic theologians' So there was the opportunity for a real 'theological dialogue, well prepared and with a sufficiently diverse representation', which could 'guarantee the objectivity of the result as far as possible'.

All in vain. On 8 March, the President officially announced the *final answer* to me. It is a technically sophisticated letter, with the evident purpose of 'justifying' a procedure by formalistically legal arguments, which were not always objectively true – a procedure for which I had requested gospel fellowship and theological rigour. In a private communication announcing this text, he had told me: 'Be certain that your writings have been carefully studied and opinions about them compared throughout these years by different experts.' I replied, also in private: 'You will understand that this way of going behind the back of the person concerned... offends not only the spirit of minimal church fellowship, but the most basic rules of serious – and dare I say – responsible dialogue'.

But the official letter, arguing that that it is not a 'trial', declares that such a dialogue is not mandatory, and gives its final reason: 'Therefore the bishops do not debate on a theological level but teach the truth of the faith that must be held to, because in their role as genuine teachers, endowed with the authority of Christ and in communion with the Roman Pontiff, "they are witnesses to the divine and Catholic truth".'

Stat pro ratione voluntas [What I want stands for a reason]. I confess that I find this mixture of levels and confusion of intentions incomprehensible. It is a practical denial of any role for the work of theologians, which St Thomas described as 'magisterium cathedrae *magistralis,'* side by side with the 'magisterium cathedrae *pastoralis*' – the *teaching* magisterium beside the pastoral magisterium– about which the current pope states: 'Theologians need the ministry of pastors of the Church, just as the Magisterium needs theologians'. Apparently, in their *specific and ecclesially original mission* of establishing, defending and explaining the credibility of the faith, theologians must say nothing of their own accord about the 'divine and Catholic truth'. They totally lack the quality of 'genuine teachers' and are deprived of sacramental participation in 'Christ's authority'.

I end this account with the final words of my private reply: 'Now it is done, let's see how we can minimize the damage. I hope you will understand that as I said to you before, I shall endeavour publicly to defend my theology and my honour as a theologian. The only thing I desire is to do it in a way that accords best with the Gospel.'

Translated by Dinah Livingstone

Contributors

JOSÉ OSCAR BEOZZO was born in Santa Adélia, São Paulo, Brazil in 1941. He studied philosophy in São Paulo (1958–60), theology at the Gregoriana in Rome (1960–4), and social sciences and communication at Leuven, Belgium. He was awarded a doctorate in social history at São Paulo in 2001. He is General Coordinator of the Ecumenical Centre for Evangelization and Popular Education in São Paulo; in charge of São Benedito parish; a member and former President of CEHILA (Commission for Studies in the History of the Church in Latin America) (1974–2011). He teaches post-graduate missiology studies at the São Paulo Theological Institute. His many publications include: *Leis e Regimentos das Missões—Política Indigenista no Brasil*,1983; *A Igreja do Brasil: de João XXIII a João Paulo II, de Medellín a Santo Domingo,*[2] 1996; *A Igreja do Brasil no Concílio Vaticano II: 1959–1965,* 2005; co-author of *Tecendo memórias, gestando futuro–História das Irmãs Negras e Indígenas Missionárias de Jesus Crucificado,* 2009; he is managing editor of the collection *Curso de Verão de São Paulo,* 1988–2012.

Address: J. Oscar Beozzo
Rua Dr Mario Vicente 1108
Vila Dom Pedro – Ipiranga
Seminário João XXIII – Fundos
São Paulo SP 04270—001, Brazil
Email: jbeozzo@terra.com.br

MARIA CLARA LUCCHETTI BINGEMER holds a doctorate in systematic theology from the Gregorian University in Rome and is currently Professor of Theology at the Pontifical Catholic University of Rio de Janeiro, Brazil. Her recent publications include: *Jesus Cristo: Servo de Deus e Messias glorioso,* 2009; *Simone Weil: a forca e a fraqueza do amor,* 2007; *Um rosto para Deus?*, 2005; and numerous articles in Brazilian and other journals.

Contributors

Address: Prof. Dr Maria Clara Bingemer
Pontifícia Universidade Católica do Rio de Janeiro
Depto. de Teologia (TEO)
Rua Marquês de São Vicente, 225,
Edificio Cardeal Leme 11 andar
Caixa Postal: 38097 22453-900 - Rio de Janeiro - RJ – Brazil
Email: agape@puc-rio.br

MARY E. HINES grew up near Boston, MA. She holds a PhD in systematic theology from the University of St Michael's College, Toronto, Canada and is Professor of Theology at Emmanuel College in Boston. Among her publications are *What Ever Happened to Mary?*; *The Transformation of Dogma: An Introduction to Karl Rahner on Doctrine; The Cambridge Companion to Karl Rahner* (which she co-edited), and numerous articles on ecclesiology, feminist theology and theology of Mary. The ongoing reception of Vatican II is a particular research interest. She has served on the Board of Directors of the Catholic Theological Society of America and on the Anglican–Roman Catholic Consultation in the United States (ARCUSA).

Address: Department of Theology and Religious Studies
Emmanuel College
400 The Fenway
Boston, MA 02115
USA
Email: hines@emmanuel.edu

PETER HÜNERMANN was born in Berlin in 1929. He studied philosophy and theology in Rome. He was ordained priest in 1955, and was awarded a doctorate in theology in 1958. He was Professor of Dogmatic Theology at Münster and Tübingen universities, Germany, and has been professor emeritus since 1997. He has taught periodically in Latin America and in the United States. He is Honorary President of the European Society of Catholic Theology. His many publications include his own works and editions, such as the fortieth edition of *Enchiridion symbolorum, definitionum et declarationum de rebus fidei et morum* and a major commentary on Vatican II.

Contributors

Address: Prof. Peter Hünermann
Engwiesenstrasse 14
D-72108 Rottenburg
Tel. 07073/3725; Fax 07073/910253
Email: Peter.huenermann@uni-tuebingen.de

MARTIN MAIER SJ, was born in 1960 in Messkirch, Germany. He entered the Society of Jesus in 1979. He studied philosophy, theology and music in Munich, Paris, Innsbruck and San Salvador. From 1995 to 2009, he was a member of the editorial board of *Stimmen der Zeit*, and editor-in-chief from 1998 to 2009. Since 2009, he has been Rector of the Berchmanskolleg in Munich. He has undertaken regular teaching assignments at the Universidad Centroamericana in San Salvador and at the Centre Sèvres in Paris. His publications include: *Pedro Arrupe–Zeuge und Prophet*, Würzburg, 2007; with Gianni La Bella (ed.): *Pedro Arrupe–Generaloberer der Gesellschaft Jesu. Neue biographische Perspektiven*, Freiburg im Breisgau, 2008; *Oscar Romero–Kämpfer für Glaube und Gerechtigkeit*, Freiburg im Breisgau, 2009.

Address: Kaulbachstrasse 31a,
D-80539 Munich, Germany
Email: martin.maier@jesuiten.org

ALBERTO MELLONI was born in Reggio Emilia, Italy, in 1959. He studied in Bologna, at Cornell University (New York) and in Fribourg (Switzerland). He is Professor of Christian History at the University of Modena–Reggio Emilia. He holds the title of Unesco Fellow in religious pluralism and peace of the University of Bologna, and he is Secretary of the Giovanni XXIII Foundation for Religious Science in Bologna. His recent publications include: *Papa Giovanni. Un cristiano e il suo concilio*, Turin, 2009, and *Pacem in terris. Storia dell'ultima enciclica di papa Giovanni*, Rome & Bari, 2010. He was managing editor of the *Dizionario del sapere storico-religioso del Novecento*, Bologna, 2010, *Cristiani d'Italia*, Rome, 2011, and the series *Corpus Christianorum–Conciliorum Oecumenicorum Generaliumque Decreta*, Turnhout, 2007.
Address: Alberto Melloni

Contributors

Via F. Crispi 6
40121 – Reggio Emilia
Italy

JOHN W. O'MALLEY SJ is a University Professor at Georgetown University, Washington, USA. He writes especially on the religious culture of early modern Europe. Of his eight highly-esteemed monographs the best-known is *The First Jesuits*, Cambridge, MA, 1993. In 2008 he published *What Happened at Vatican II*, Cambridge, MA, and this year *Trent: What Happened at the Council*, Cambridge, MA.

Address: Box 571200,
Washington, DC 20057-1200
USA

AGBONMKHIANMEGHE E. OROBATOR SJ received his PhD from the University of Leeds and is currently Provincial Superior of the Eastern Africa Province of the Society of Jesus, as well as lecturer in theology at Hekima College Jesuit School of Theology. He specializes in ecclesiology and ethics. His recent publications include: *Faith Doing Justice: A Manual for Social Analysis, Catholic Social Teachings, and Social Justice*, with Elias O. Opongo, 2007; *Theology Brewed in an African Pot*, 2008; *Reconciliation, Justice, and Peace: The Second African Synod* (editor), 2011.

Address: Agbonkhianmeghe E. Orobator, SJ
Loyola House
P. O. Box 21399
Ngong Road,
Nairobi 00505, Kenya

ANDRÉS TORRES QUEIRUGA was born in 1940, and was until his retirement in 2011 Professor of Philosophy of Religion at the University of Santiago de Compostela, Spain. He describes his main concerns as applying the idea of 'the God who creates out of love' to the main theological topics and commitment to an 'evangelical democratic' renewal of Church order. His many published works include *Constitucion y evolucion del dogma*,1977; *Recuperar la salvacion*, 1977, 2001; *Creo en Dios Padre*, 1998; *Recuperar la creacion*, 1977; *Fin del cristianismo premoderno*, 2000; *Repensar la resurreccion*, 2003; *Esperanza a pesar del mal*, 2005; *Repensar la revelacion* , 2008, revised ed. 1977; *Repensar el mal. De la ponerologia a la teodicea*, 2011.

Address : Facultade de Filosofía
15782 Santiago de Compostela, Spain
Private: O Curraliño, 23-G. 15705
Santiago de Compostela. Spain
Email: torresqueiruga@gmail.com

GIUSEPPE RUGGIERI was born in Pozzallo, Catania, Italy in 1940 and is Emeritus Professor of Fundamental Theology in the Faculty of Theological Studies at Catania. He has taught at the Gregorian University in Rome and in the Faculty of Catholic Theology of the University of Tübingen, Germany. He is one of the founders of the review *Communio* and was in charge of the Italian edition for the first four years. He is a member of the advisory board of *Concilium* and managing editor of the review *Cristianesimo nella storia*. His many publications include: *Cristianesimo, chiese e vangelo*, Bologna, 2002, and *La verità crocifissa. Il pensiero cristiano di fronte all'alterità*, Rome, 2007.

Address: Giuseppe Ruggieri
Piazza Dante 32
95124 – Catania
Italy
Email: rotger@tin.it

GÉRARD SIEGWALT was born in 1932 and formerly taught dogmatic theology in the Faculty of Protestant Theology of the University of Strasbourg. He is the author of *Dogmatique pour la catholicité évangélique*, in five volumes, each with two half-volumes, which appeared from 1986 to 2007 in Paris and Geneva (*I: Problématique et méthodologie théologiques*; II: *Sociologie théologique*; II: *Cosmologie théologique*; IV:

Anthropologie théologique; V: *Théologie théologique*). His most recent publication is Lise d'Amboise & Fritz Westphal, *Entretiens avec Gérard Siegwalt: Dieu est plus grand que Dieu. Réflexion théologique et expérience spirituelle*, Paris, 2012.

Address: Gérard Siegwalt
25 rue Sainte Cécile
67100 Strasbourg
France

JON SOBRINO, SJ was born to Basque parents in Barcelona in 1938 and educated in Spain, Germany, and the USA, where he obtained a Master's degree in engineering. He joined the Society of Jesus in 1956 and since 1957 has been a member of the Central American Province and lived mainly in El Salvador. He is Professor of Theology and Director of the Monsignor Romero Centre at the Catholic University of Central America in San Salvador. He is joint editor with Ignacio Ellacuria, the Rector of the university, murdered in 1993, of *Mysterium Liberationis: Fundamental Concepts of Liberation Theology*, 1993. Among his many books translated into English are the two-volume Christology *Jesus the Liberator*, 1993, and *Christ the Liberator*, 2001. Recent works include *Cartas a Ellacuría*, 2004; *Fuera de los pobres no hay salvación. Pequeños ensayos utóico-proféticos*, 2007.

Address: Unversidad Centroamericana,
Centro Monsenor Romero, Apartado (01)
168 San Salvador, El Salvador
Email: jsobrino@cmr.uca.edu.sv

CHRISTOPH THEOBALD SJ, teaches fundamental theology and dogmatic theology in the Faculty of Theology in Paris (Sèvres Centre) and is editor-in-chief of the review *Recherches de Science Religieuse*. He is the author of numerous publications on the history of theology (particularly on Vatican II), systematic and practical theology and aesthetics. Recent works among his many publications include: *Le Christianisme comme style. Une manière de faire de la théologie en postmodernité,* vols 1 & 2,

Paris, 2007; *Transmettre un Evangile de liberté,* Paris, 2007; *'Dans les traces' de la constitution 'Dei Verbum' du concile Vatican II,* Paris, 2009; *La réception du concile Vatican II, vol. 1: Accéder à la source,* Paris, 2009.

Address: P. Christoph Theobald
15 rue Monsieur
F-75007 Paris
France

FELIX WILFRED was born in Tamilnadu, India in 1948. He was for many years Professor at the State University of Madras, and President of the Faculty of Arts in the same University. He was a member of the International Theological Commission of the Vatican, when Cardinal Joseph Ratzinger was the chairperson. As visiting professor, he has taught at the Universities of Frankfurt, Münster, Nijmegen, Boston College, Ateneo de Manila and Fudan University, Shanghai. He had the singular honour of having been appointed by the Government of India as the first holder of its newly-established Chair of Indian Studies at Trinity College, Dublin. His researches and field studies today cut across many disciplines in humanities and social sciences. His latest major publication is on *Asian Public Theology* (2010).

Address: Asian Centre for Cross- Cultural Studies, 40/6*A* Panayur Kuppam Road, Panayur, Sholinganallur Post, Chennai – 600119, India.
Email: felixwilfred@gmail.com

CONCILIUM
International Journal of Theology

FOUNDERS
Anton van den Boogaard; Paul Brand; Yves Congar, OP; Hans Küng;
Johann Baptist Metz; Karl Rahner, SJ; Edward Schillebeeckx

BOARD OF DIRECTORS
President: Felix Wilfred
Vice Presidents: Erik Borgman; Diego Irarrázaval; Susan Ross

BOARD OF EDITORS
Regina Ammicht Quinn (Frankfurt, Germany)
Maria Clara Bingemer (Rio de Janeiro, Brazil)
Erik Borgman (Nijmegen, The Netherlands)
Lisa Sowle Cahill (Boston, USA)
Dennis Gira (Paris, France)
Hille Haker (Frankfurt, Germany)
Diego Irarrázaval (Santiago, Chile)
Solange Lefebvre (Montreal, Canada)
Eloi Messi Metogo (Yaounde, Cameroon)
Sarojini Nadar (Durban, South Africa)
Daniel Franklin Pilario (Quezon City, Philippines)
Susan Ross (Chicago, USA)
Silvia Scatena (Reggio Emilia, Italy)
Jon Sobrino SJ (San Salvador, El Salvador)
Luiz Carlos Susin (Porto Alegre, Brazil)
Andres Torres Queiruga (Santiago de Compostela, Spain)
Marie-Theres Wacker (Münster, Germany)
Felix Wilfred (Madras, India)

PUBLISHERS
SCM Press (London, UK)
Matthias-Grünewald Verlag (Ostfildern, Germany)
Editrice Queriniana (Brescia, Italy)
Editorial Verbo Divino (Estella, Spain)
EditoraVozes (Petropolis, Brazil)
Ex Libris and Synopsis (Rijeka, Croatia)

Concilium Secretariat:
Asian Centre for Cross-Cultural Studies,
40/6A, Panayur Kuppam Road, Sholinganallur Post, Panayur, Madras 600119, India.
Phone: +91- 44 24530682 Fax: +91- 44 24530443
E-mail: Concilium.madras@gmail.com
Managing Secretary: Jayashree Narasimhan

www.ingramcontent.com/pod-product-compliance
Lightning Source LLC
Chambersburg PA
CBHW051403290426
44108CB00015B/2136